Pals, Pets, Pigs, & Potatoes!

Jennie Eble, Paige Lee, and
April Koger

&

School Books Press

www.schoolbookspress.com

Pals, Pets, Pigs, & Potatoes!

ISBN: Softcover 978-1-949888-33-1

Pals, Pets, Pigs, & Potatoes!

Contents

Introduction

Welcome to the wonderful world of *Pals, Pets, Pigs, and Potatoes*!

Pals, Pets, Pigs, and Potatoes was produced as a service-learning project by Cleveland State Community College English Composition II students in a unique partnership with Taylor Elementary School first grade students. The two groups of talented students wrote and illustrated the amazing stories making up this delightful collection.

Literacy and creativity are important aspects of growing up, but we don't always realize how important they are for adult lives. In the same way that reading is necessary, we often need creative thinking to function well in our jobs, homes, and families. As with any skill, practice helps performance. This project was challenging at times for the college students, but they will certainly not forget this exercise in creativity. For the children who participated, we hope they can keep using those creative skills.

For our readers, we hope this book of fun short stories will bring grins and giggles. Read on to meet the loveable and zany characters of *Pals, Pets, Pigs, and Potatoes!*

Blue Jeans and Moo-lawn Travel the World

Justin Gregory and Kami Taylor

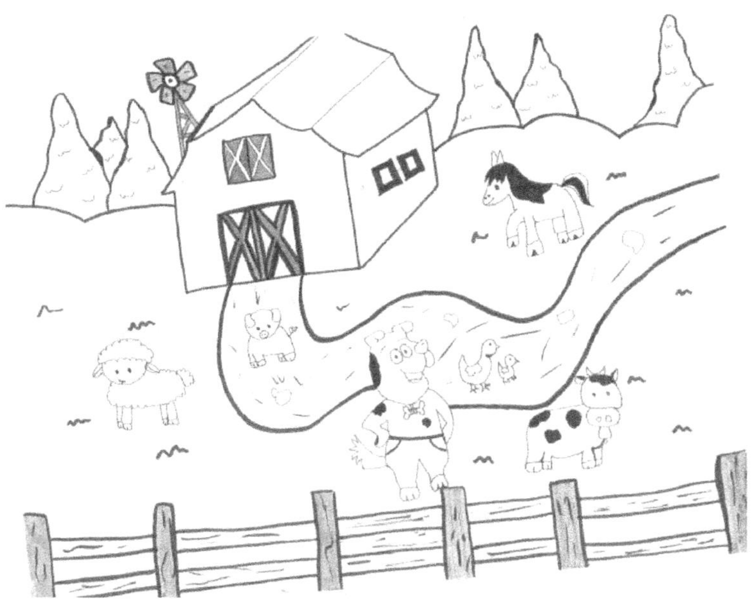

Out in the country on a farm far away, there lived a dog named Blue Jeans. He worked on the farm every day keeping the animals safe and happy.

Blue Jeans loved every one of his farm friends dearly, but there is one that Blue Jeans is very close to; Moo-lawn.

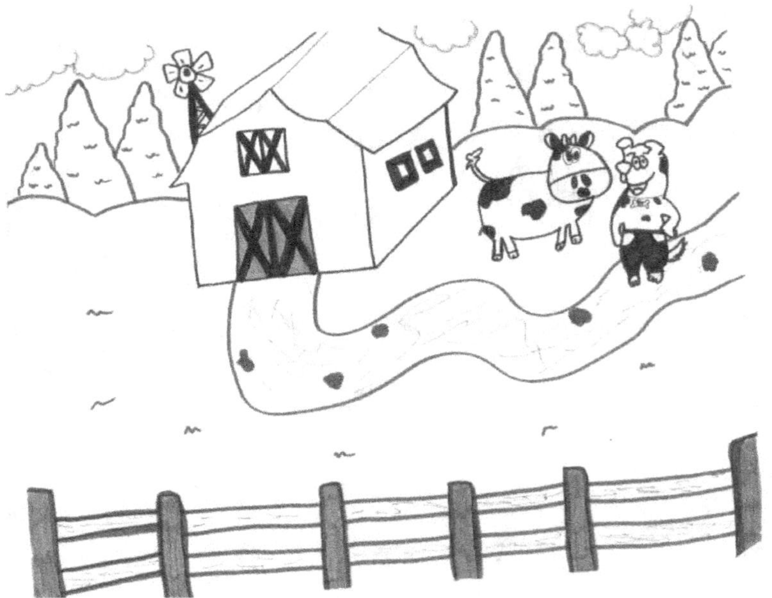

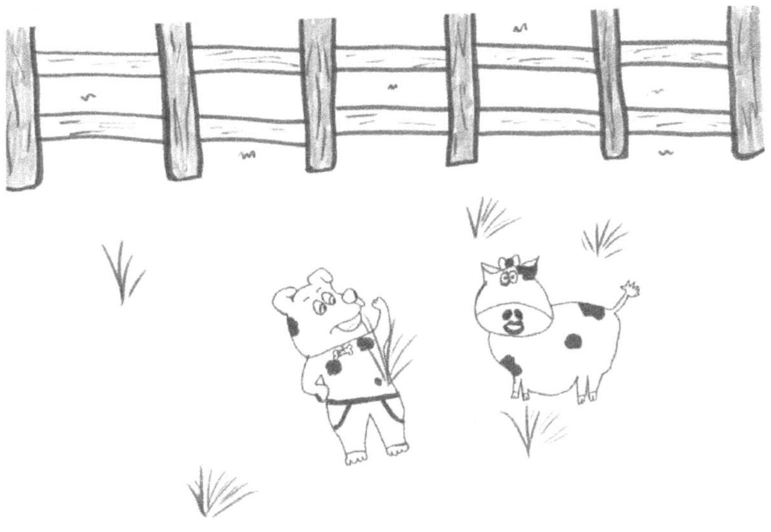

Moo-lawn is one of the oldest cows that lived on the farm. Moo-lawn decided that she had enough of the farm. She wanted to travel the world. Blue Jeans tried to convince her to stay, but Moo-lawn convinced Blue Jeans to go with her.

As the night grew close, Blue Jeans and Moo-Lawn traveled to the closest airport. They had to travel through the many fields of other farms, and they passed through the spooky forest.

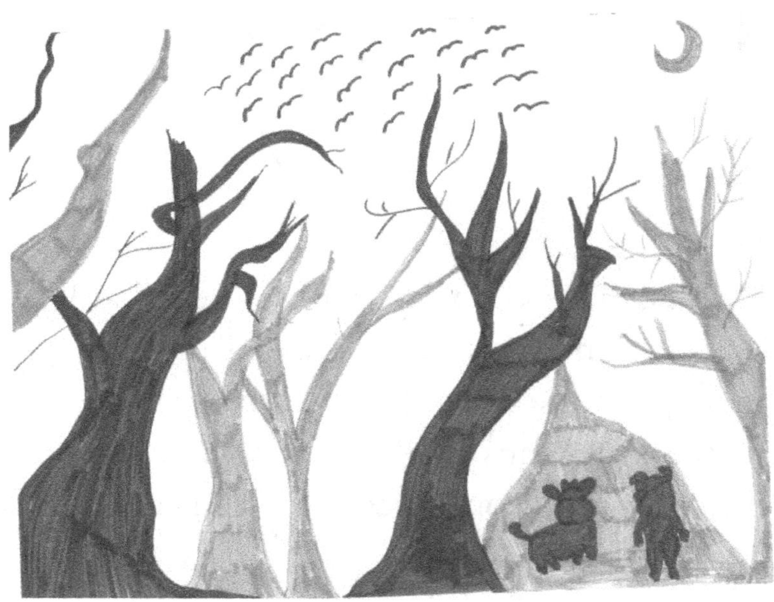

Blue Jeans and Moo-lawn finally made it to the airport. After buying their plane tickets for Australia, they went through airport security. After they got through security, they went to get aboard their plane.

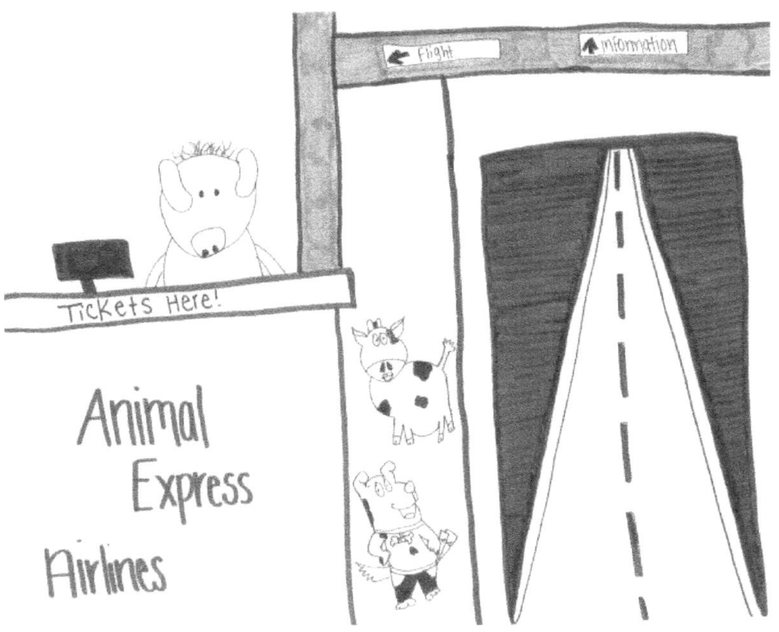

After boarding the plane, Blue Jeans and Moo-lawn finally find their seats. Surprisingly, their seats were in first class. They got as many dog treats and grass clumps as they wanted!

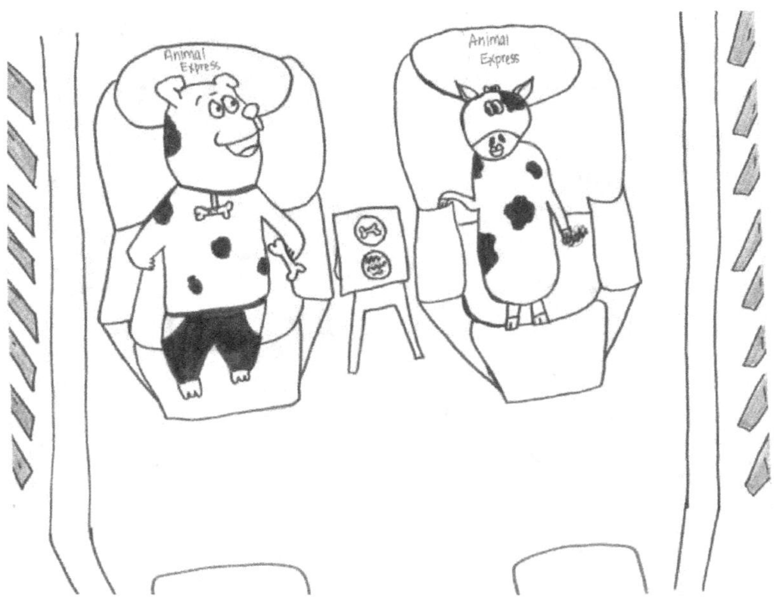

While on their long journey, Blue Jeans and Moo-lawn enjoyed all of the delicious food, long naps, and watching their favorite movies on the plane.

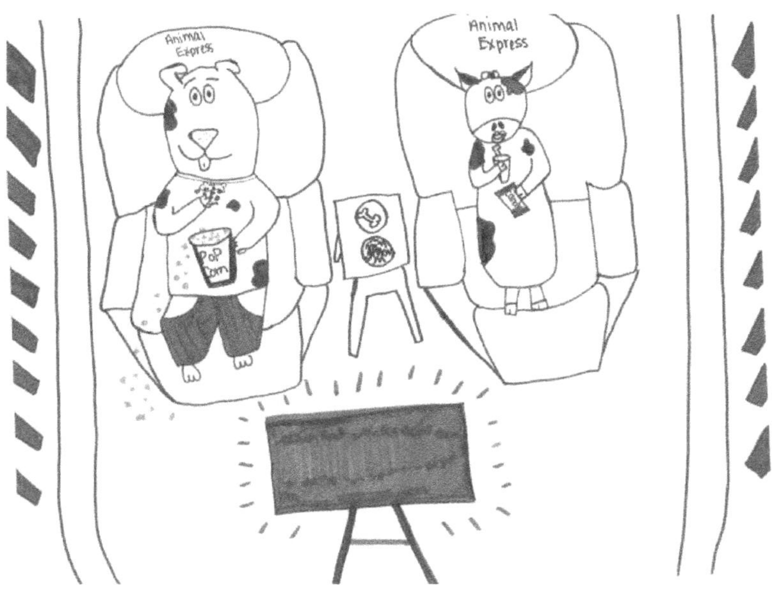

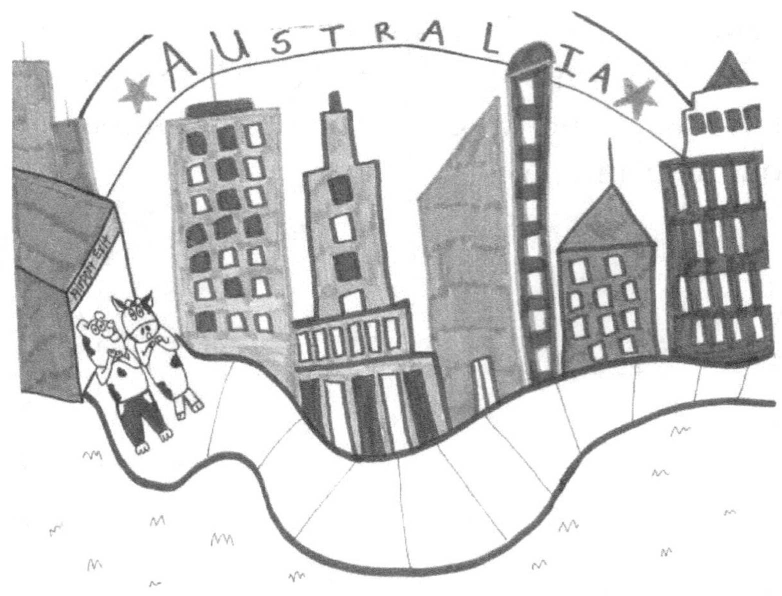

After a long ride, Blue Jeans and Moo-lawn finally arrive in Australia. They ran off the plane as quick as they could to see the beautiful city of Australia.

Blue Jeans and Moo-lawn decided that they would like to do some sight-seeing around Australia. They got to see the many lakes, oceans, skyscrapers, and even the Sydney Harbor Bridge.

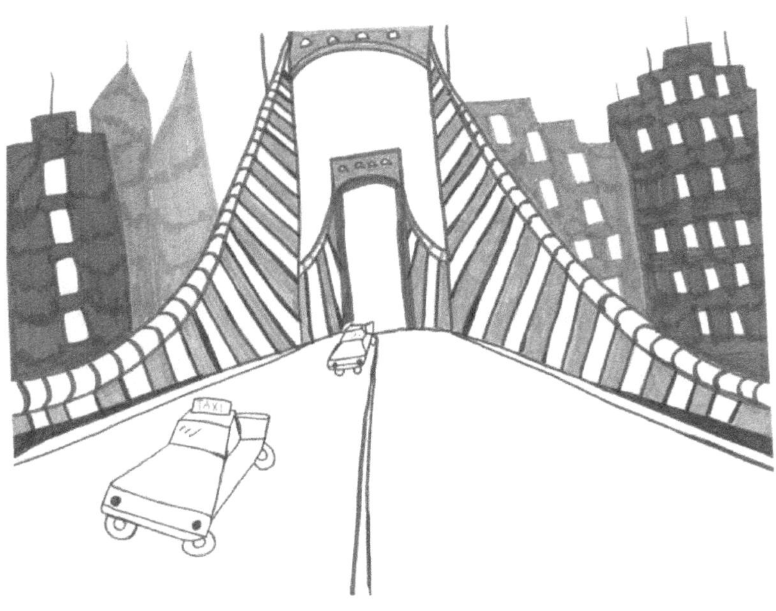

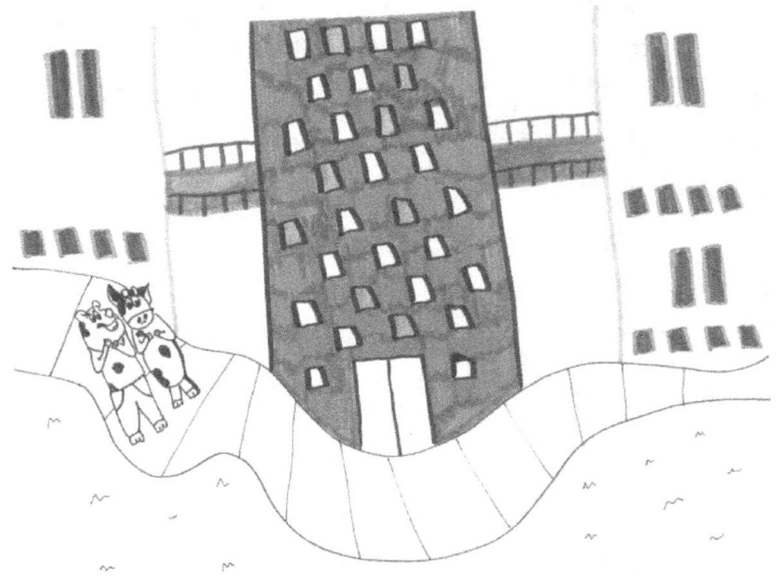

After touring Australia, Blue Jeans and Moo-lawn began to feel homesick. Australia did not have fields, pastures or friends and family like home. After a long day of sightseeing, Blue Jeans and Moo-lawn both agreed that this was not the place for them.

They finally came to the conclusion that there is no place like home. So, they went to the airport to purchase their plane tickets, and they boarded the plane to head home. They were so excited to return back to their many fields and pastures, and they could not wait to see their friends and family.

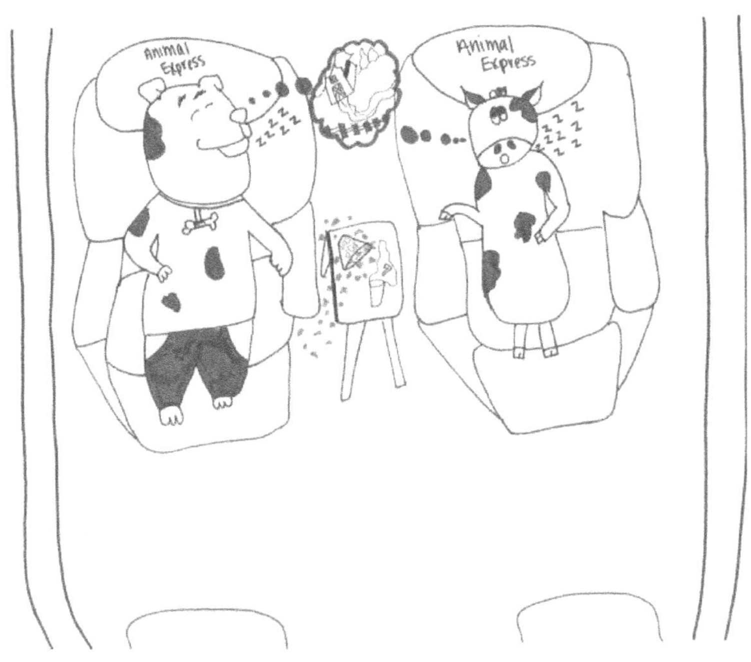

After the long ride back home, the plane finally landed, and they ran off as fast as they could. They could not wait to see everyone. They ran all the way back to the farm, and they were reunited with all of their friends and family. They realized that no matter how cool or fun the rest of the world looked to them; there was no place like home.

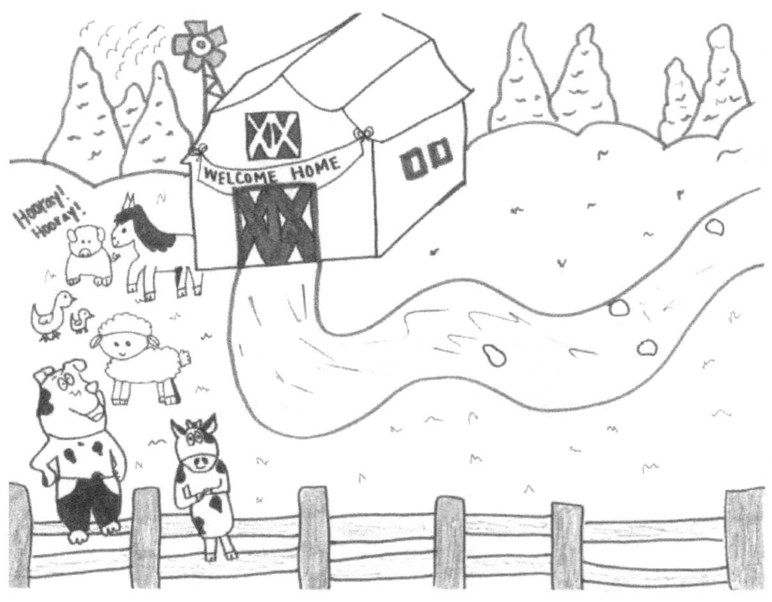

A Super Halloween

Jared Bean and Sara Harper

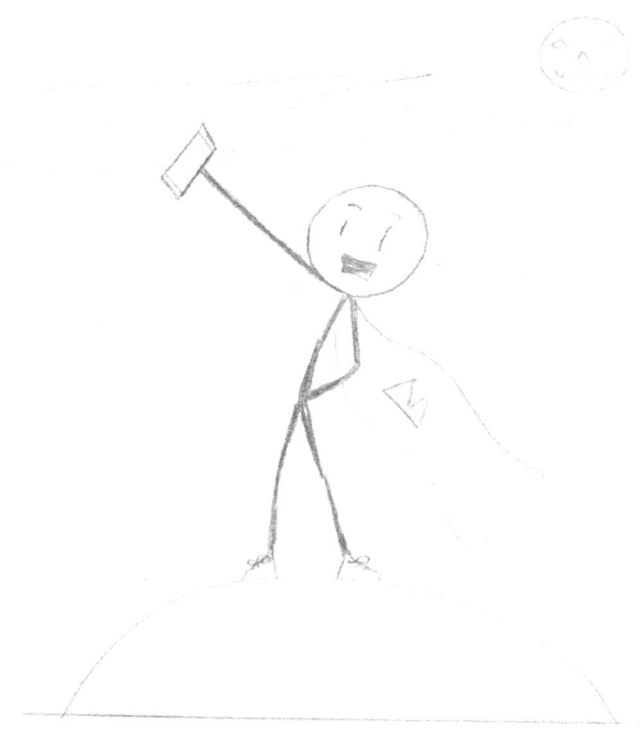

Tommy couldn't wait for his first Halloween, he sat at the kitchen table thinking about all the candy he was going to get this year. "All I have to do is find a really cool costume" he thought. Just then his mom started talking to him, "Why don't you make some friends and go trick or treating with them, that could be a lot of fun." "I just started school I don't really know anybody to trick or treat with," Tommy answered.

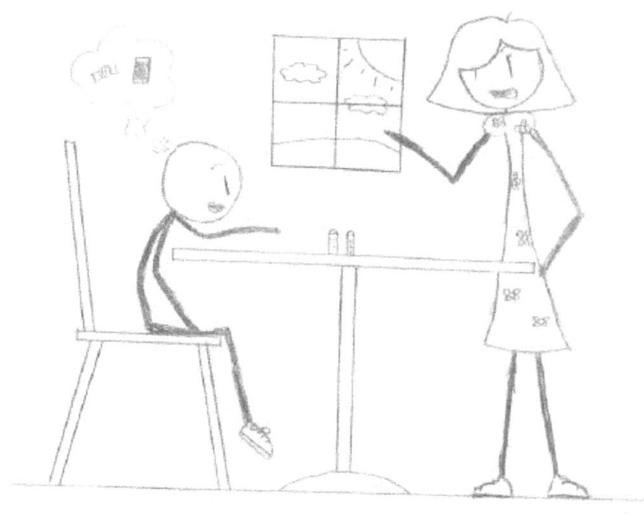

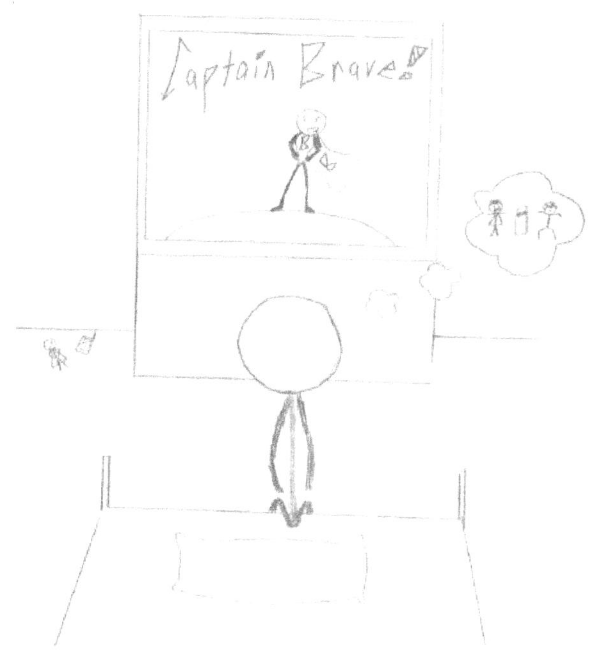

Tommy went to his room, moving to a new town was hard and he missed his old friends. But Tommy still had his favorite superhero, Captain Brave. As he watched Captain Brave fight off the bad guys he thought about what he wanted to be for Halloween. He thought about what the three kids he'd met at school the day before said they were going to dress as, there was a vampire, a zombie, and a ghost.

The next day while at school, Tommy made a list of what he wanted to be for Halloween on a piece of paper. First, he wrote a firefighter then thought about red and how he hated it. After, he wrote a soccer player but started thinking about how he didn't like sports. Finally, he wrote down a zoo keeper and then thought about how he didn't like animals.

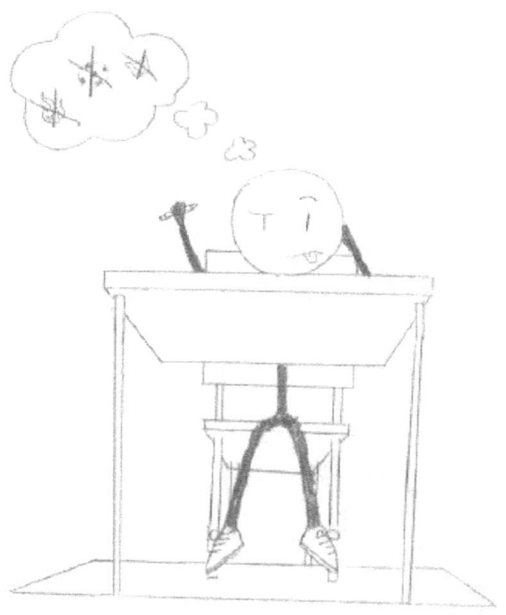

That night at dinner, Tommy's mom talked more about how he should make friends and dress up, "I have made a few friends" he said, "there's Anna, Luke, and James, they're all dressing up for Halloween and going trick or treating." "Well, we better find you a costume soon or you won't be able to go." said his mother. "Can I go to my room now?" asked Tommy. "Yes but be thinking about what you want to dress as because Halloween is in a couple of days," answered his mom.

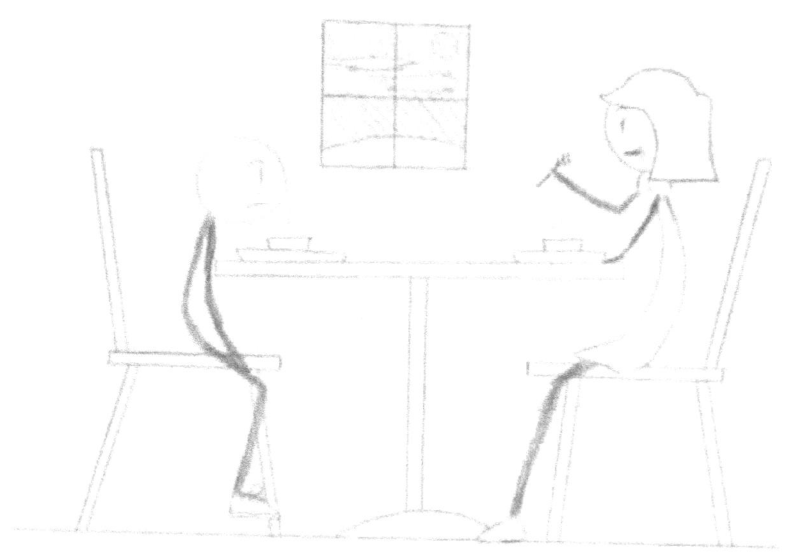

That night Tommy tossed and turned until he finally was asleep and started to have a dream. In his dream, he was at school and it was Halloween. When Tommy looked around his classroom all of his friends were dressed in Halloween costumes, but when Tommy looked at himself, he didn't have a costume on. Tommy's heart started beating fast and he started sweating. One of the kids pointed at him and started laughing, Tommy didn't know what to do. The room was spinning and then he woke up to the sound of his mother's voice telling him to wake up. I have to get a costume soon," Tommy whispered to himself.

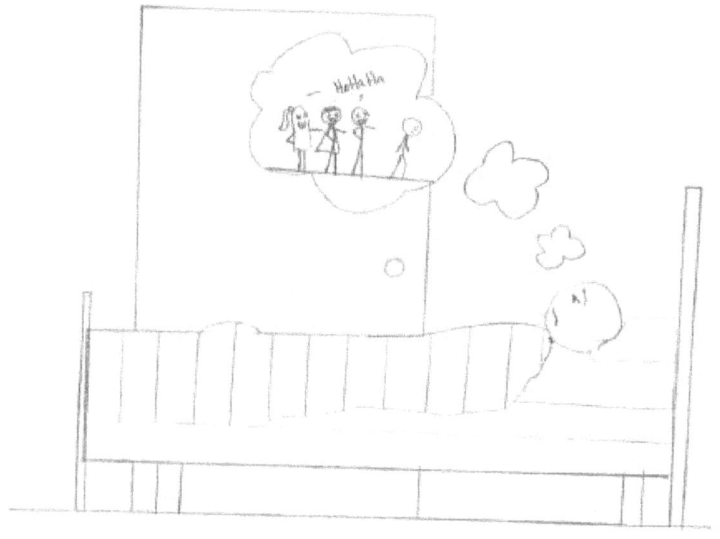

The next day, Tommy asked his mother if he could go to the store and look for a costume with her. “Yes, that sounds like a really good idea. Hopefully you’ll find something you like,” said his mom. Tommy nodded and followed her out the door. When they got to the store he went straight to the costumes, but what he found there was scary. There were all kinds of masks and different costumes. Tommy hid behind his mom. “I don’t think I want to dress up for Halloween anymore,” Tommy said looking up at his mom.

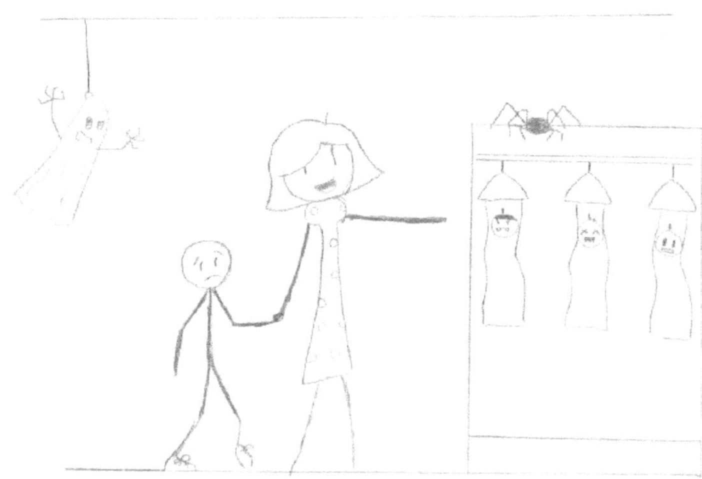

When they got home from the store, Tommy went straight to his room. He was so ashamed that he had gotten scared, the only thing he could hope for was that none of his friends had seen him hiding. Tommy was about to give up on Halloween until his mom walked in and sat on the end of his bed. She started to say, "I know it's hard to celebrate when you don't know many people and you don't have a costume, but I think you should try, it could help you make friends."

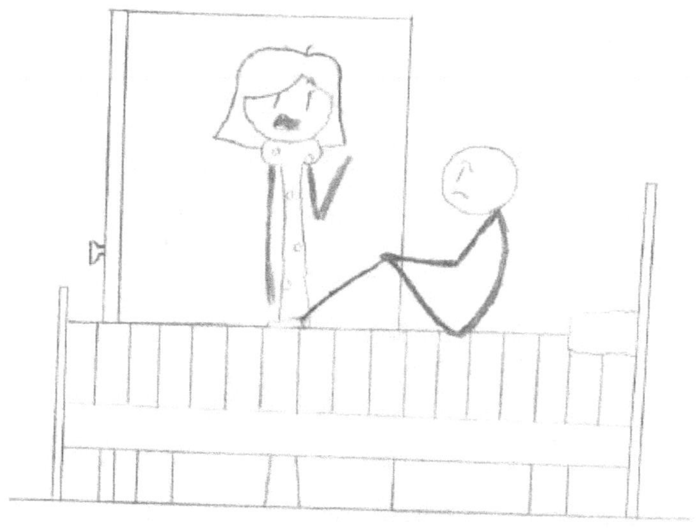

“I know,” Tommy said. He looked down at the floor. His Captain Brave comic was laying on the ground at the side of his bed. Suddenly he got an idea. If he wanted to be brave then he should dress up like his hero, Captain Brave, it was such a good idea.

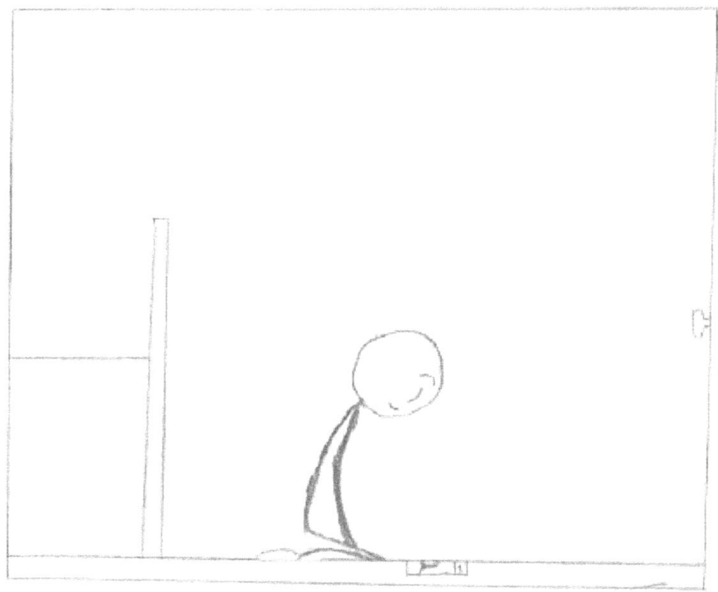

"MOM! I HAVE AN IDEA!" Tommy yelled, "I WANT TO BE CAPTAIN BRAVE!" "That's wonderful honey, we'll go to the store tomorrow and find you a costume." Tommy's mom replied. Tommy stayed up all night thinking about what his costume would look like and what his friends would think of it. The next day, he was so happy he could hardly contain it. His mom took him to the store after school and they found a Captain Brave costume just like what Captain Brave wore in the TV show.

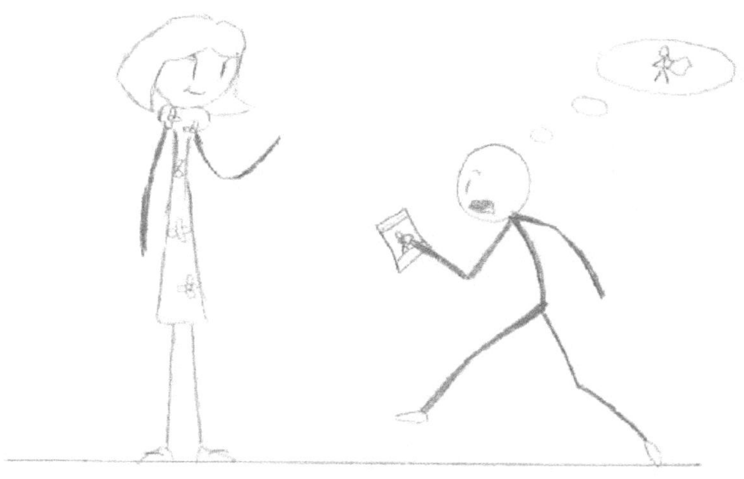

The next night, Tommy put on his costume and smiled into the mirror. “You look so cute honey, have fun trick or treating with your friends” said his mom. When Tommy met with Anna, Luke, and James they were all in costume too, and looking scary. They took one look at his costume and loved it. “I watch that show every week,” said Anna. “I love the comic,” said Luke. “I want to be Captain Brave,” said James. “Thank you guys, let’s go get some candy” said Tommy. They all laughed and started trick or treating, “I can’t wait until next year!” said Tommy with a big smile across his face.

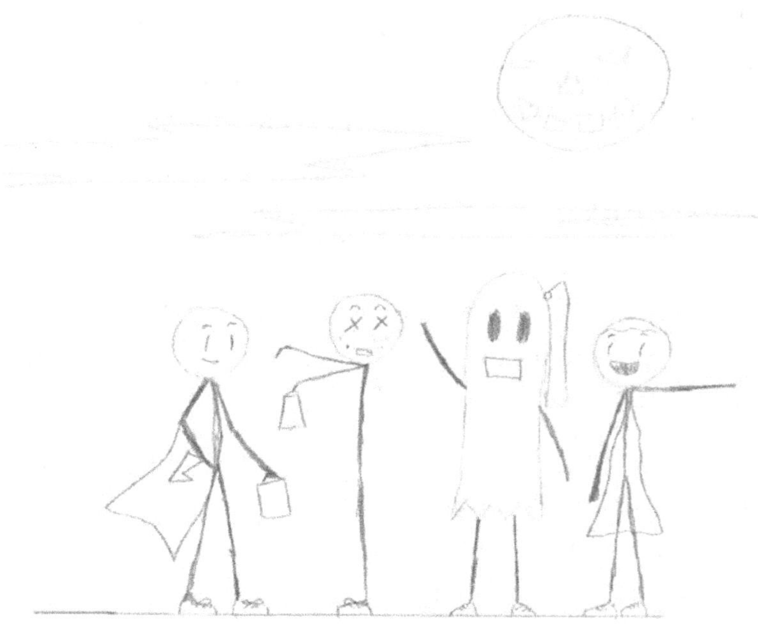

The Pumpkin and The Spider

Jacquelyn Hannah and Harlie Chastain
Illustrated by Megan McElhinney

In a little town called Yellville, PA, Sara and Xander had decided they were going to participate in their school's annual costume contest that was held on all hallows eve. All school employees and students were allowed to participate and dress in a costume. Sara was going to be a spider and Xander was going to go as a pumpkin.

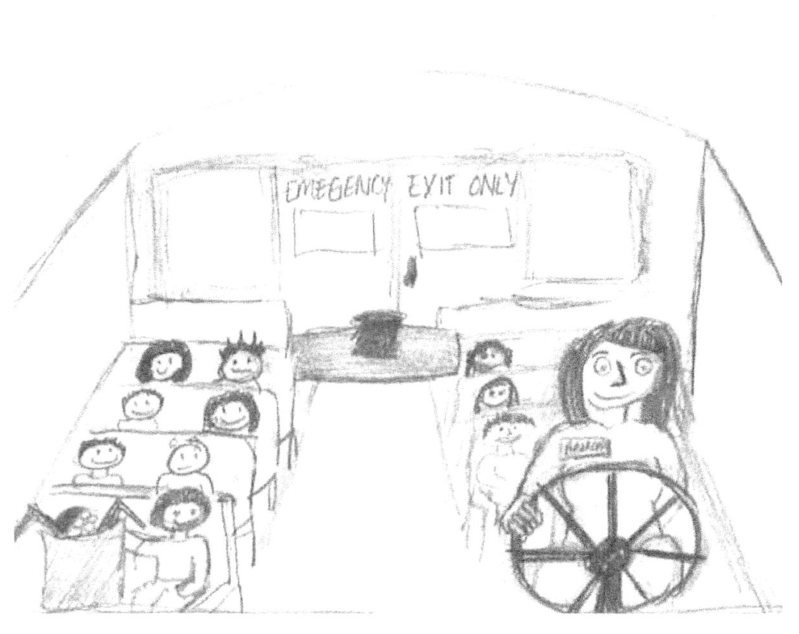
EMEGENCY EXIT ONLY

At lunch, Sara was so excited that she got into her spider costume a whole hour early.

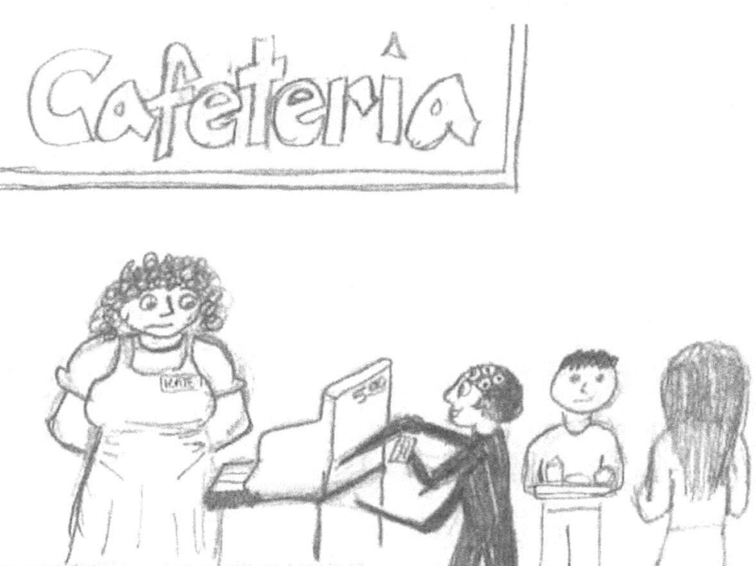

When the time came for the winners to be announced Sara and her brother Xander were asked to stand up on stage. It was a tie between the two of them for best costume!

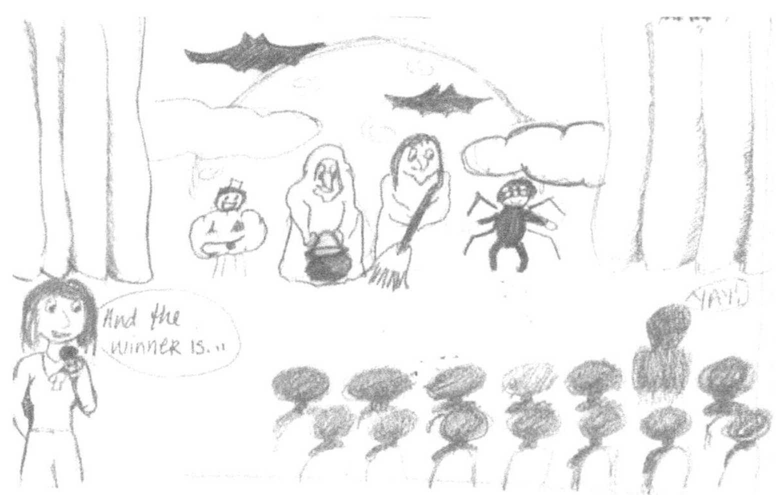

The worst costume award went to the three sister employees who had each dressed as witches.

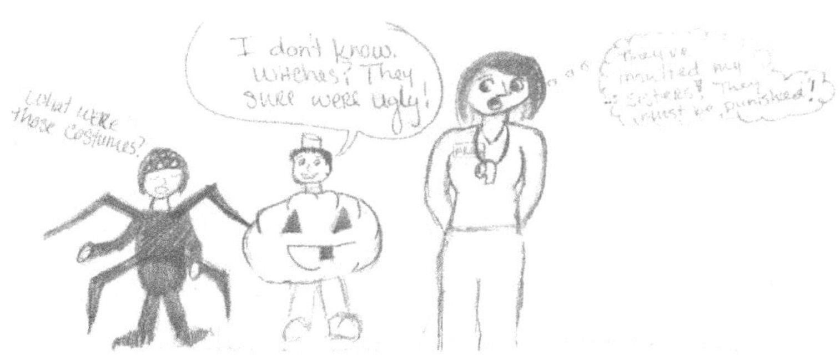

"What were those costumes. . . witches?", asked Sara.

"Whatever they were they were pretty ugly!", replied Xander.

Without realizing it the two siblings had been over heard by one of the sisters, the gym teacher. Mrs. Gym Teacher knew then that the kids would need to be taught a lesson in calling people ugly.

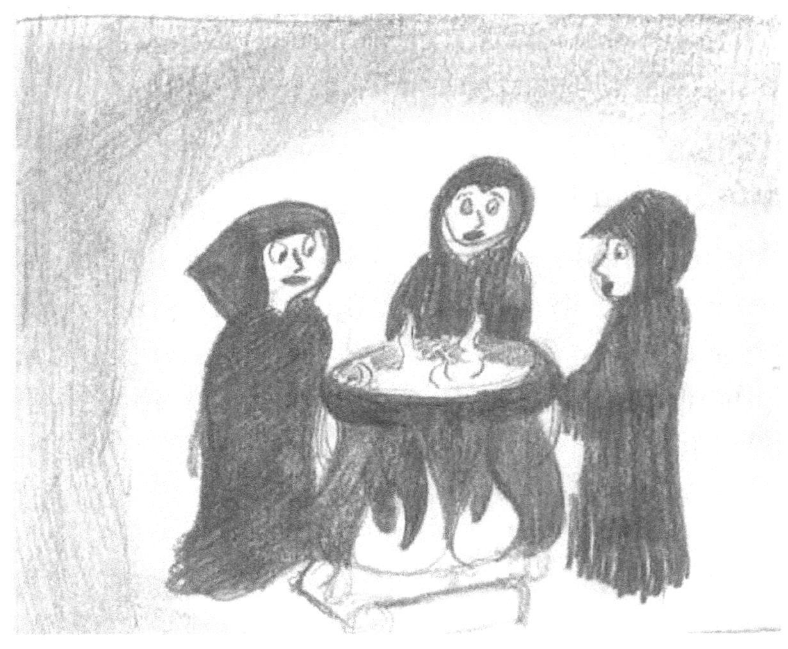

Unbeknownst to the town, the sisters were real witches! So that night they brewed up a spell. When the clock strikes twelve and the night turns into Halloween the children will turn straight into the costumes they were so proud of.

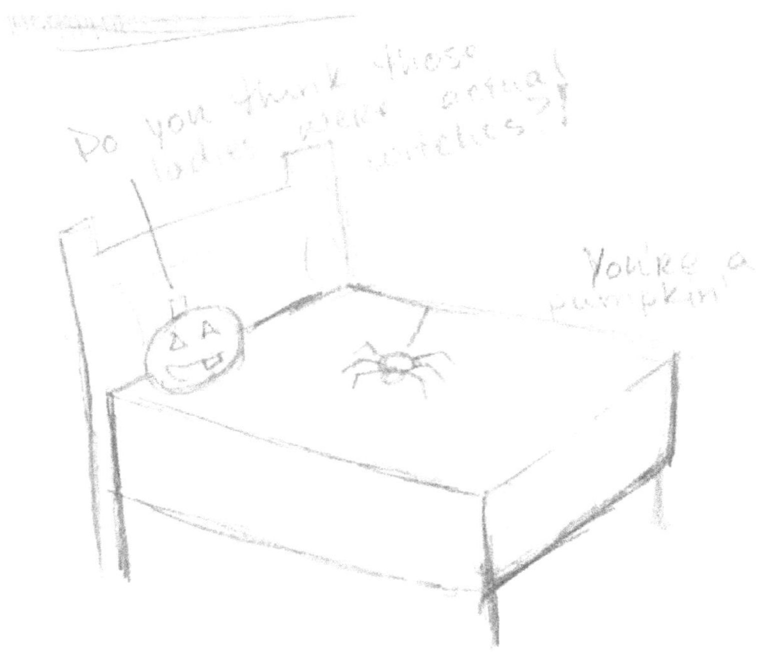

Sara woke up first and raced down the hallway to Xanders room.

“Xander! Wake up! . . . YOU’RE A REAL PUMPKIN?!. . . I’M A REAL SPIDER!!”, she said in a panic.

Xander was sitting on the bed when Sara had crawled under the door, thinking. “Do you think those witches that won worst costumes were actual witches?!

The brother and sister realized that they should’ve been nicer to the witch sisters. They decided to head back to the gym at school to see if the witches were still there cleaning up. They were determined to apologize. Neither of them enjoyed being an ugly pumpkin or spider!

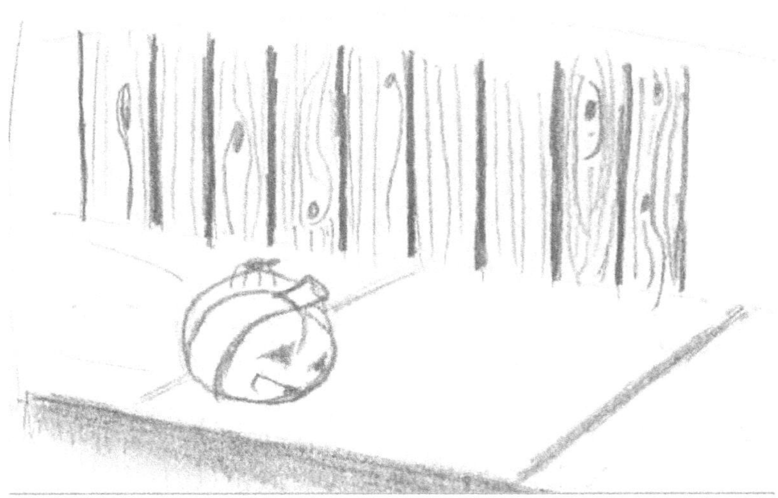

When they arrived at the gym they saw that Mrs. Gym Teacher was in fact there helping clean up. She noticed the pumpkin with the spider riding a top it and walked over to them.

“Well hello, children,” she said with a half grin on her face.

Xander, not wanting to waste any time said, “We are so so so so so so so sorry Mrs. Gym Teacher.”

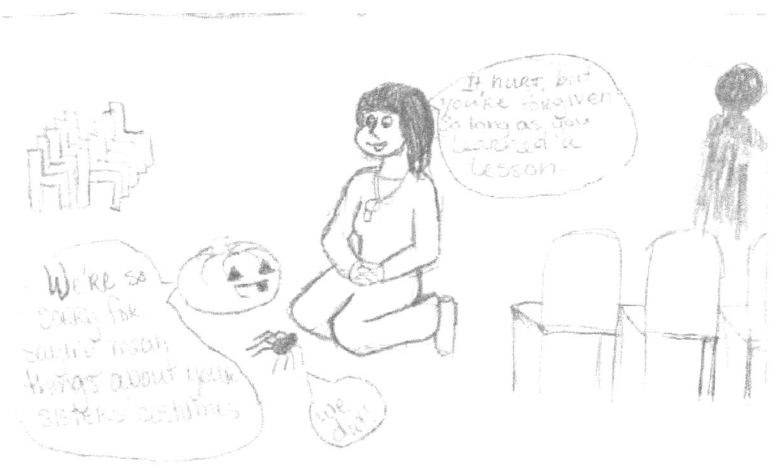

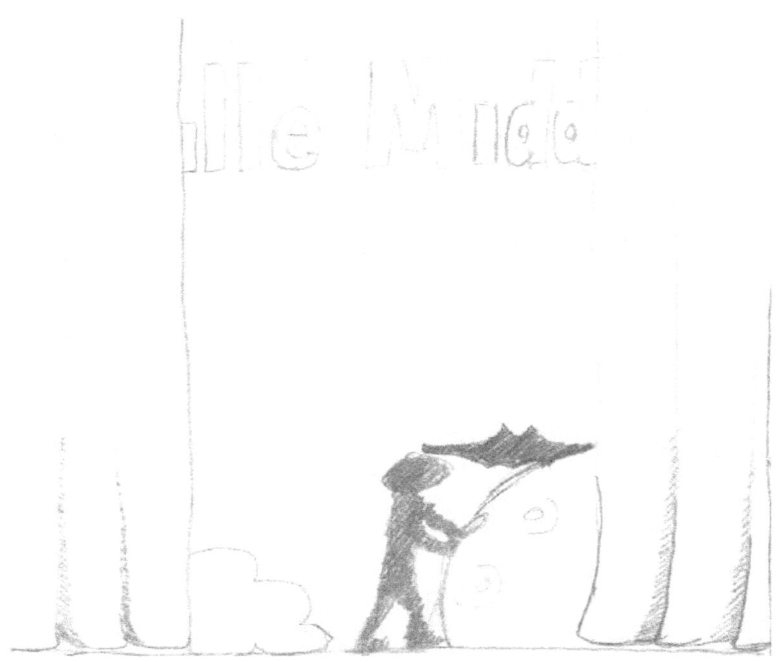

“We deeply regret calling you and your sisters ugly. It must have been very hurtful for you to have heard,” said Sara.

“Do you think you have learned your lesson, children? Just because you do not like the way someone looks does not mean they are ugly.” Mrs. Gym Teacher looked down at the little pumpkin and tiny spider. “I suppose this little lesson has gone on long enough,” she said and then clapped her hands three times.

And with the third clap of her hands Sara and Xander turned back into their real selves.

“Mrs. Gym Teacher?”, asked Sara. “Would you and your sisters like to join me and my brother tonight for some Halloween trick or treating? We would love to show your costumes around our neighborhood!”

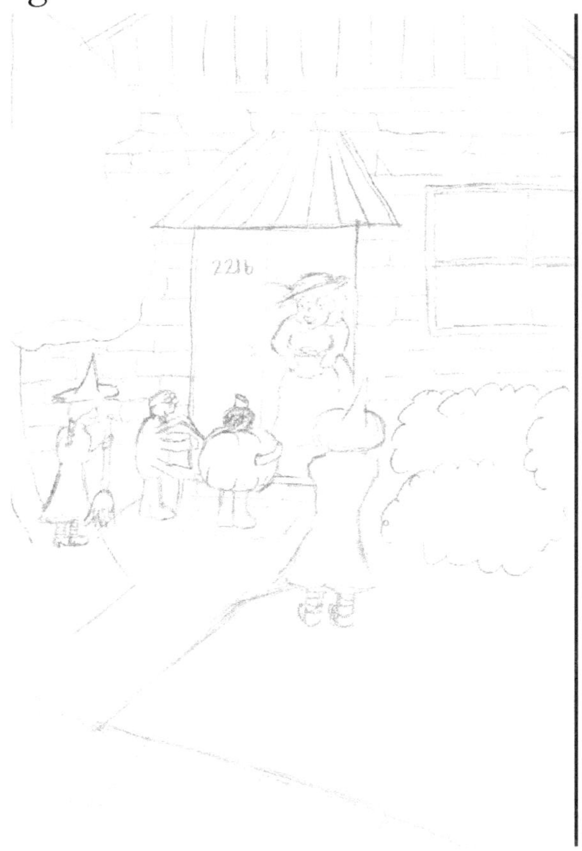

And with everyone being back to themselves again and a lesson learned - they all went trick or treating.

Mr. Catstein Goes to Cairo

Ivy Falls and Oleksandra Paladian

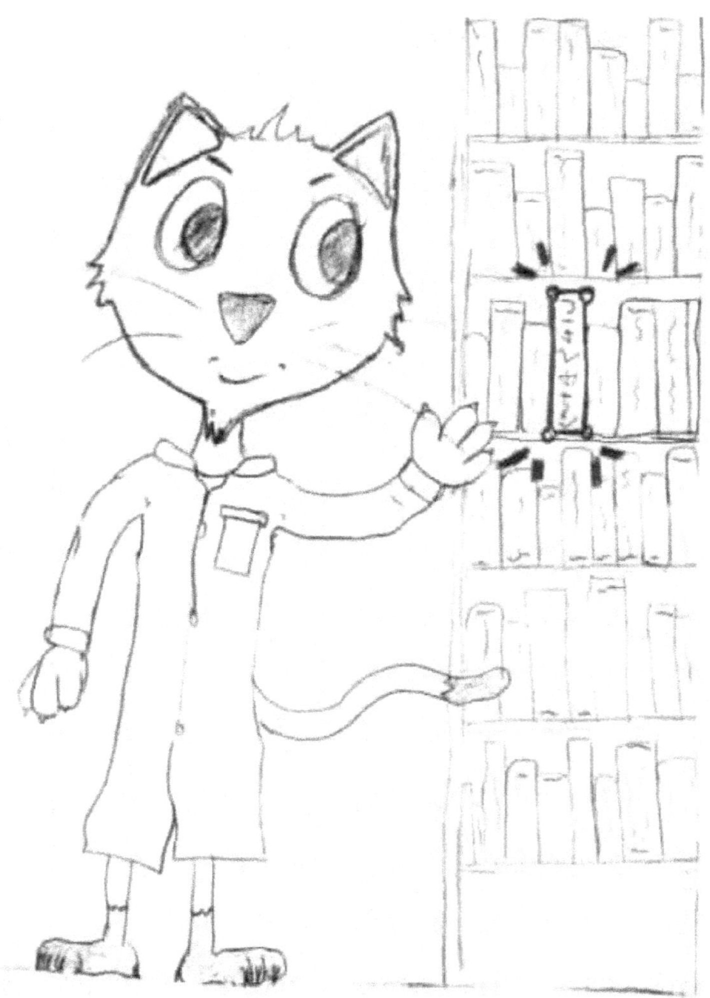

On a rainy Sunday afternoon, Mr. Catstein was studying at the Oxford library in England.

He was a professor of archeology, which means he studied the treasures from the past. The day at the library was quite an adventure for the professor, though he was getting tired from searching various books all day long. Before he left, Catstein ended up in the Egyptian section of the library. Upon looking at all the books that described ancient Egypt, Mr. Catstein was puzzled. He had a feeling that a piece of history was missing. In fact, he was looking for an ancient library that has been lost for thousands of years. The legend was that an ancient stone can lead anyone to the forgotten library and all the treasures that lie within. The first step was to find the stone. Most of the ancient papyrus was transported to the Oxford, so that was why he was looking for it here in Oxford. Hours and hours went by and Mr. Catstein had not found anything. The professor got even more tired and he sat down at the bottom of the bookcase, where his thoughts went on a walk through his old memories. He was thinking about his discoveries of ancient treasures from all different cultures and times, the pride of displaying them in the museum, and the honor of having been the one who found the lost pieces of history. As he was about to give up on his quest, a strange black book fell from the top shelf right next to his feet. There were no markings on it. The book had a leather cover and was very worn from many years of use. Mr. Catstein picked it up and opened the mystery book. The pages inside were not written in English, they were written in the hieroglyphics, which was the writing from the old times in Egypt. Also, there were different diagrams and strange symbols that the professor could not understand. As he was looking through the book, an old piece of paper fell out. It did not have any symbols or hieroglyphics, but it showed a map of Cairo. More specifically, the map showed a diagram of the great pyramids. Mr. Catstein understood immediately what this strange piece of paper meant, it was a treasure map to the ancient stone. Excited by his discovery, he hurried back home, packed everything that he needed, and traveled all the way from Oxford, England to Cairo, Egypt.

Upon arriving in Cairo, Egypt, Mr. Catstein packed a small backpack of all essential items that included the map and the strange black book full of hieroglyphics. Disguised as a tourist, the professor traveled to the great pyramids. He distracted the tour guide and came closer to the pyramid; his next mission was to find his way in. All the sudden, Catstein felt a strange heat coming out of the backpack, it was his black book. As he opened the book, one of the far-right blocks of the pyramid slid right out. Intrigued by this discovery, the

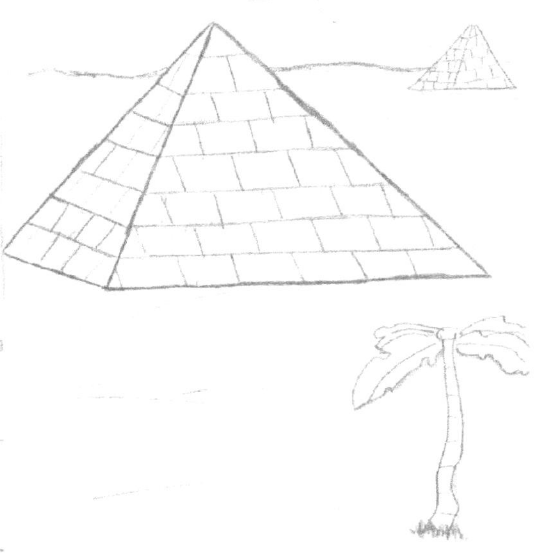

archeologist slipped inside. It was dark inside, so Mr. Catstein pulled out a box of matches and struck a match, which made him see a torch on the left side of the wall. After lighting the torch, the pathway was clearly visible, so the professor started going down the path. The hallway was low and narrow, which was slightly sloping downward. Upon coming to the end of it, Mr. Catstein saw a message written on the wall, "He who shall dare awake Pharaoh Baughkma, will be cursed when touched". The professor did not think much of the message, he thought it was one of those superstitious alerts that the ancient people left to scare everyone away. With that thought, he looked around to find a way to continue his journey. Again, the mysterious black book started getting hot in his hand and the side wall slid open to another dark, low, and narrow hallway. Mr. Catstein followed it; however, as he stepped only a few steps into it, an ax slipped from the side of the wall, following another one. Panic set into the professor and he rushed to get through the sharp metallic blades. As he ran away, the treasure map that was in his pant pocket fell and was left in the hallway of swinging blades. Mr. Catstein entered a big room that had a lot of different markings on them. Even though he was an expert in hieroglyphics, the symbols were too worn out to be read easily, so the professor had set off to cross the enormous room. At the end of it, there was another hallway. Fear sank into him as he was expecting another scene of swinging blades. Prepared, he walked into the hallway cautiously, only to find a set of stairs that descended him farther down. As he reached the other landing, there were strange symbols on the floor that moved magically, with a sickly green glow coming out of them. Again, the black book started getting warmer and it fell open on the page with the diagram where the pieces were arranged in the right order. Mr. Catstein did the same thing to the moving pieces. Upon finishing them, they made a hissing sound. All the sudden, the floor crumbled and the professor fell through. The world went swirly and dark.

31

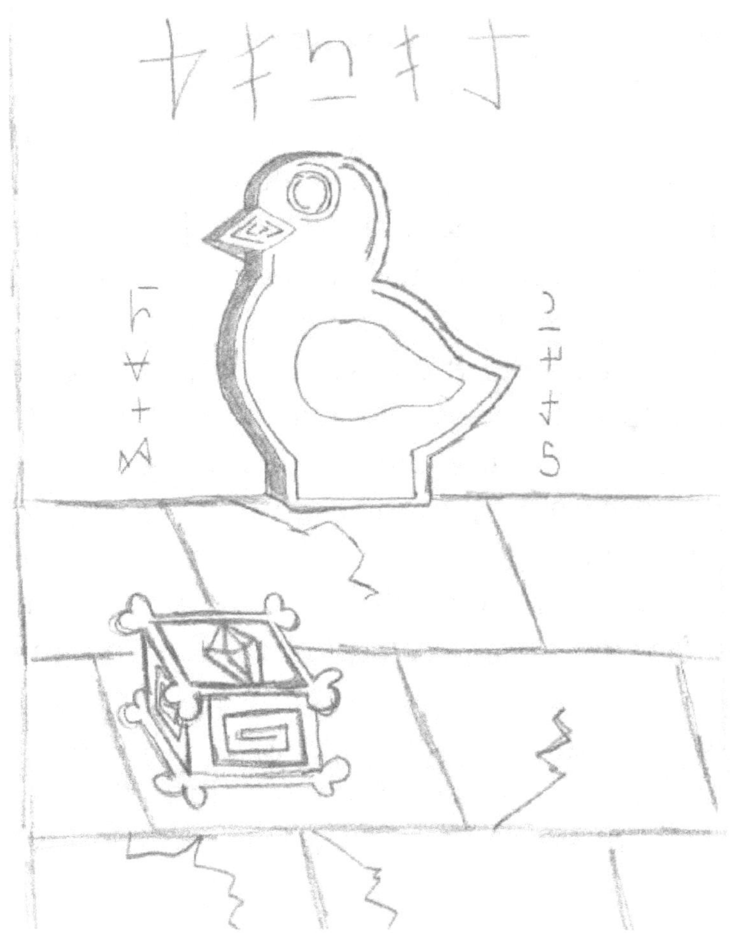

When he woke up, Catstein found himself in a tomb with gold walls and diamond floors. The room was well lit, as if someone just lit it up with all the torches. It seemed like the room did not age at all, everything looked brand new, except of the sarcophagus in the middle of the room. A sarcophagus was a coffin used in ancient Egypt, usually reserved for very important people. What Mr. Catstein saw on top of it, he could not believe his eyes, was the very same stone that he was on the hunt for. Forgetting the formal warning on the wall, he grabbed the stone. Suddenly, the whole room shook, and the flame flickered. The sarcophagus rumbled and cracked open revealing a mummy. It looked like a chicken, but all bandaged up. Its eyes started to glow, and the mummy arose. That was when Mr. Catstein realized that the mummy was the ancient Pharaoh Baughkma. Remembering the message on the wall, the professor set off running for his life.

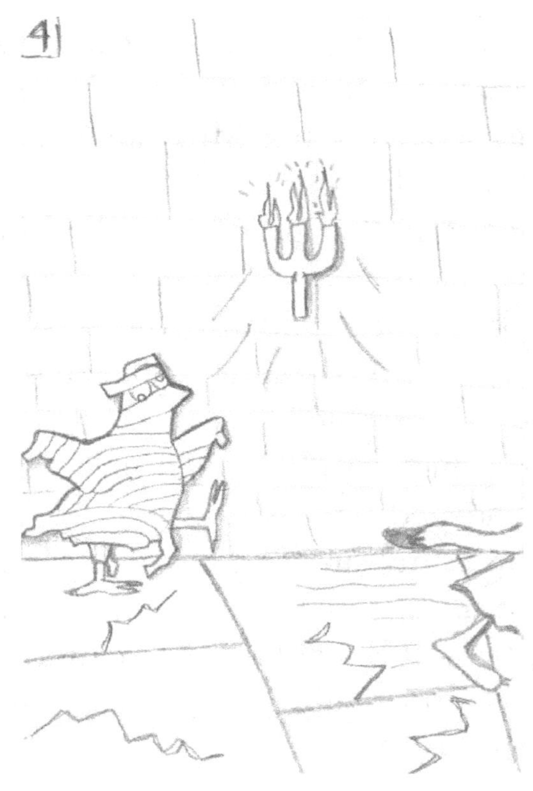

Mr. Catstein ran and ran, stumbling upon some dead ends but continued to run to what seemed nowhere.

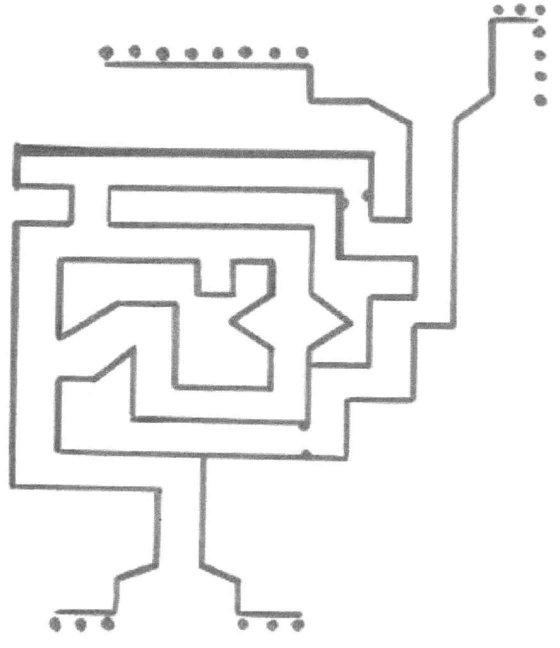

As the professor was about to lose his hope of getting out alive, he saw a big door at the end of the hallway. The door opened easily, and he slammed it shut in front of Baughkma. Mr. Catstein locked it and placed a pedestal to block the door. Once he regained his breath, he looked up to see where he was. Stunned, the professor realized that he had entered the library that he was searching for a very long time. The room contained a lot of scrolls. The archeologist was so excited, he started going through all the scrolls and he completely forgot about the mummy chicken right outside of the door. Mr. Catstein had lost track of time, he stuffed as many scrolls into his backpack as he could. The occasional thud of the door reminded him of the ancient pharaoh that he had wakened up, but he was so happy with his discoveries to be too concerned with the mummy. However, soon the sounds at the door became more rapid and Mr. Catstein started thinking about a way of getting out of that place. He took even more scrolls and started thinking. There were no other windows or doors, and the only door available was the one he blocked off. He could not go back through it; the mummy was waiting on him from the other side. That was when the black book fell again from his grasp and turned itself on the very back page. Suddenly, the ancient stone began to glow, and Mr. Catstein realized that, from the readings of the book, the legends told that the stone could teleport people. As he held the stone in his hand, the professor thought of his own library back in Oxford, to the cozy fire and the rows of books in his own home country.

Within a flash, he was standing exactly where he imagined to be, back home in his library in England. For a moment, Mr. Catstein was too stunned to realize where he was. Once he did, he was overjoyed. Immediately he contacted his fellow archeologist friends and he told them about his exciting journey and the mysterious teleportation. The stone was placed in the museum and Mr. Catstein became even more popular. However, when he got to read the scrolls that he got from the ancient library, the professor was shocked.

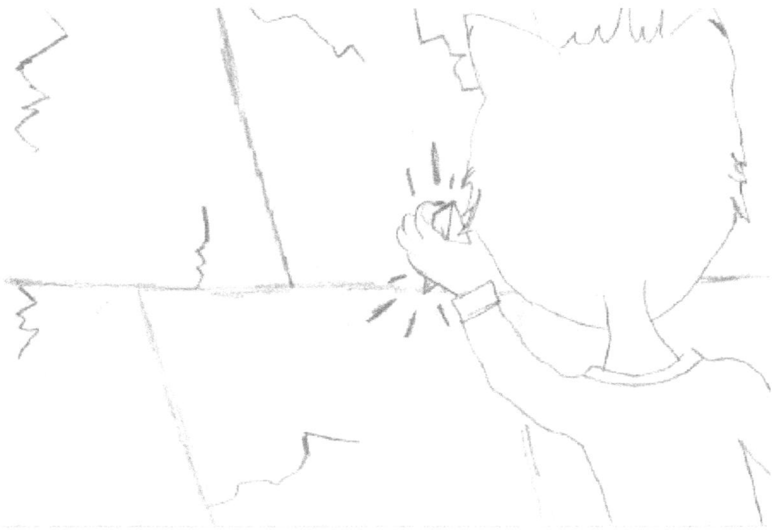

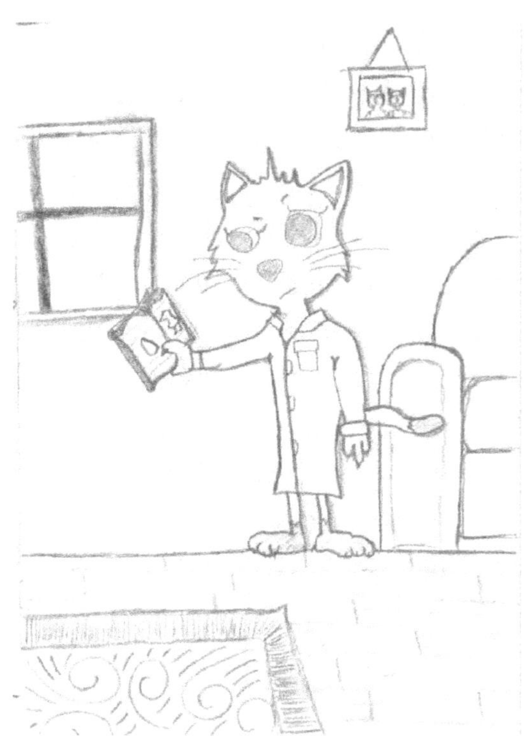

Apparently, the whole library was dedicated to the study of chickens. Everything was about chickens! The mummy, Pharaoh Baughkma, was a chicken and that was his library. No wonder the chicken was chasing after him.

Since Mr. Catstein lost the map in the hallway of blades and the black book was left in the ancient library, there was no way he could go back. All that was left is a stone, a good old story to tell, and a lot of scrolls about chickens.

The End

Parker the Pig

Karragan Rogers and Madi Denney
Illustration Assistance by Abby Eble

Parker the pig had a very big problem. He was afraid of mud! Mud was muddy, it was not any fun! Parker had boots to walk in the mud. They were yellow with ducks. They look like Dolly, his best friend, the duck. He wore them when he went to play with Dolly

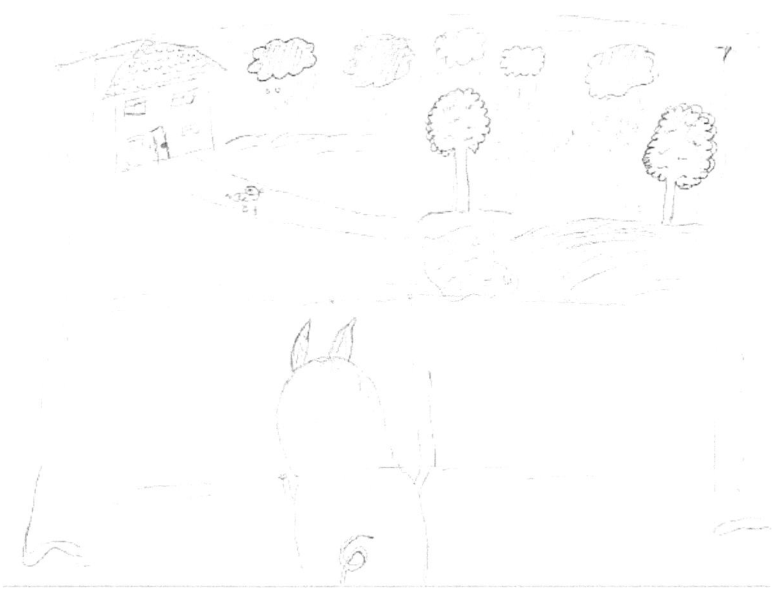

Parker kept the boots by the door, so he could go out and play with Dolly. This morning was dark, rain was falling and making a mess. Oh no! Parker can't play when it is raining. Mud came when it rained, and it was so gross!

It was so yucky outside, but Dolly was coming over to play. "My boots!" Parker oinked. "Where are my boots?" This wasn't good. It was too muddy. And he is too scared to try and play out there.

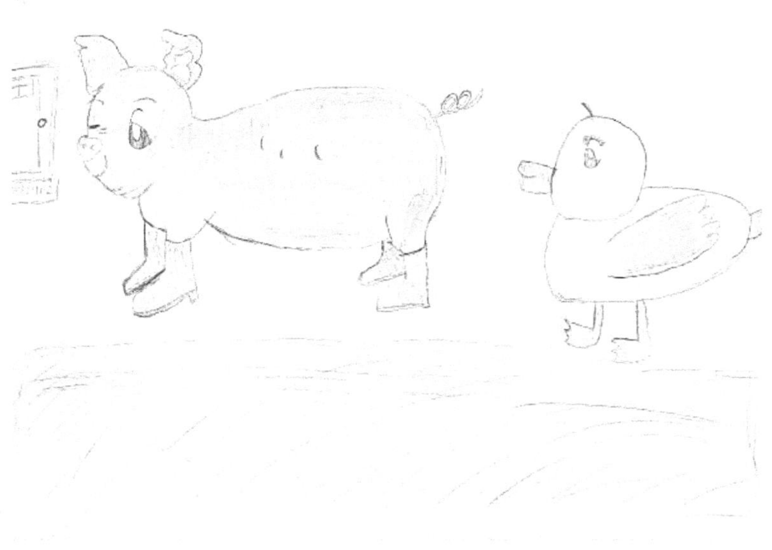

"Hey, Pig!" quacked Dolly as she peeked inside. "It's playtime! Where are you?" dolly just wanted to play, that was all. “Come outside, it’s fun!”

“I can't!” cried Parker, shaking his snout. “it’s muddy, I can’t go out!” Dolly knew this, yes, and she had a surprise. She had hidden his boots outside.

Parker snorted and followed his friend, peeking his head out of the door. He let out a squeal “eek!” and ran back in, it was too muddy, much too muddy for him.

“Don’t be afraid,” said Dolly, waddling back in. “It’s just wet dirt, and dirt is our friend.” Dolly the duck had to get Parker outside, so she finally decided to tell him that she found his boots. “They’re over here Parker! I found them, I found them!” she quacked. Parker got so excited that he had forgotten about the rain and mud, and he took off running toward his boots.

Parker the Pig was running so fast that he slipped and rolled in the mud. He finally got up and could not stop laughing, Dolly started jumping around splashing more mud on him. “You did it Parker, you did it!” They could not stop laughing.

Parker fell in love with playing in the mud that day. From that day on, Parker and Dolly played in the mud every single day after. They both have so much fun, and he never thought about using his boots again.

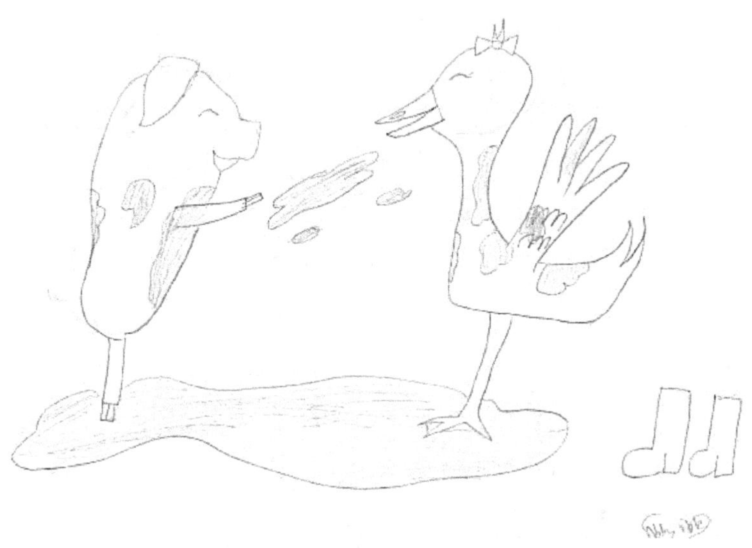

Landon's Lesson

Jill Banks

Illustrated by Abby Eble

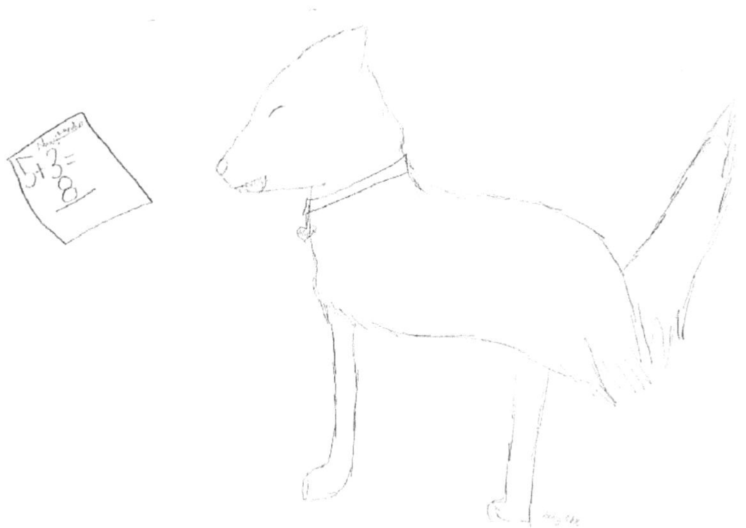

Once upon a time in a land not so far away lived a little boy named Landon. Landon loved playing football and baseball, playing video games, and playing with his toys. However, there was one thing that Landon wanted more than anything in this world. He wanted a dog. He had asked his parents for a puppy for some time now. On Christmas morning, his wish finally came true. Landon had opened all his presents when his mom said, "I have one more surprise for you." She opened the door and in ran a golden retriever puppy. Landon was so happy! This was the best day of his life. He decided to name him, Asher.

The two new pals went outside to play in the snow. They were running, jumping and having a great time. Landon built a snowman and was almost finished when he heard someone behind his say, "Now all he needs is a hat." Landon turned around and no one was there except for Asher. Landon said, "WOW! You can talk? Why didn't you tell me?" "You never asked," said Asher. That day Landon and Asher talked about everything. They had become best friends.

After Christmas break, Landon returned to school. Mrs. Eble assigned math homework the first day back. Landon hated math! He sat in his bedroom looking at all of these math problems. He didn't know the answers. "What is 3+5?" Landon said aloud. "Eight," answered Asher. Landon was amazed! Not only could his new dog talk, but he was a math whiz.

Homework was so easy over the next two weeks. Landon would simply ask Asher the math problem and Asher would tell him the answer. Landon was making 100's on all of his homework. Things were going great. One Monday morning, Mrs. Eble said, "Okay class, it's time for a math quiz." Landon was in trouble. Asher had been telling him all of the right answers, but Asher wasn't there. What was he going to do?

After recess, Mrs. Eble asked Landon to come talk to her. "You have been making perfect grades on your homework, Landon. Why did you fail this quiz," she asked? "My friend has been doing my homework," he said. Landon didn't tell Mrs. Eble that his friend was actually his dog. "Cheating is not acceptable!" said Mrs. Eble. "You will stay in and do your math homework while the rest of the class goes outside to play. You can start going to recess with the class again when you have shown me that you are doing your work on your own."

That night Landon told Asher what happened. "I can help you learn how to do your math work." said Asher. "I will not give you the answers, but I will help you learn how to solve the problems by yourself." Landon and Asher spent the evenings studying math. Landon learned how to do his work all by himself. His grades were back to being 100s and this time he was the one doing the work. Landon got every answer right on Mrs. Eble's next quiz. He learned that cheating was not right. Now Landon was making the best grades in his class thanks to his dog Asher.

Spuddicus

Sydney Corum

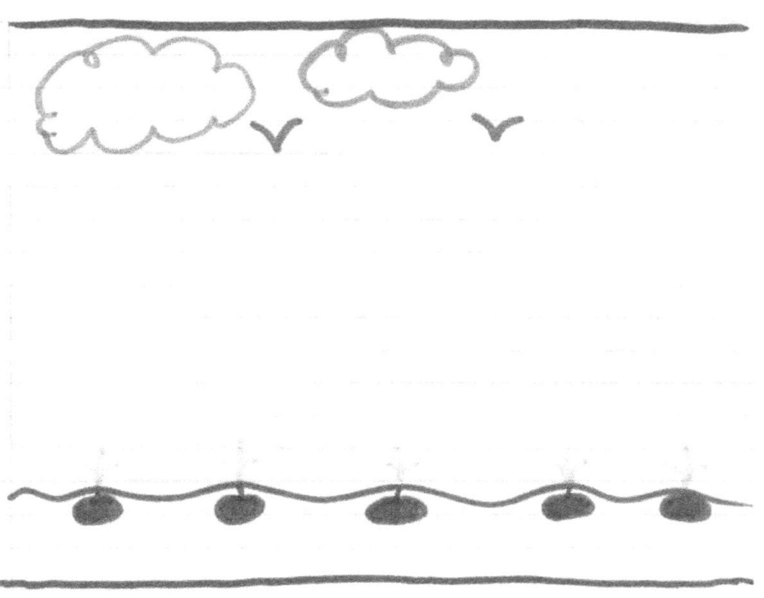

Every morning, there were chores to do on the potato farm. Tina would get out of bed, put on her potato pants, and go to work. There were lots of potatoes on the farm.

This particular morning, Tina saw something very big walking around in the field, and she heard a loud "ROAR!"

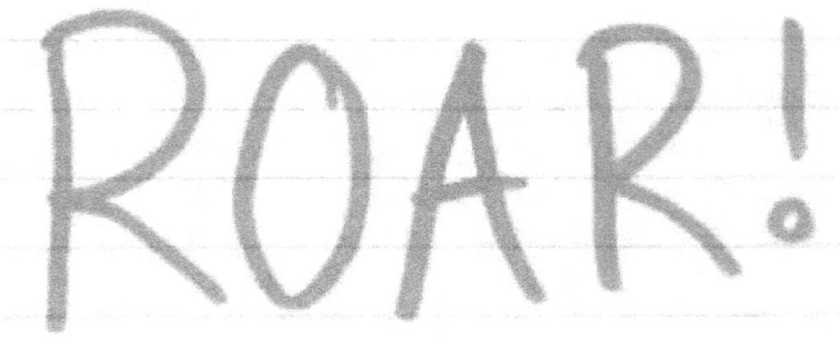

Oh no! What in the world made that noise? It certainly wasn't a potato. Or was it?

"Hello, little girl," said the giant potato who was much taller than Tina.

"H....h....hello, there," she replied timidly.

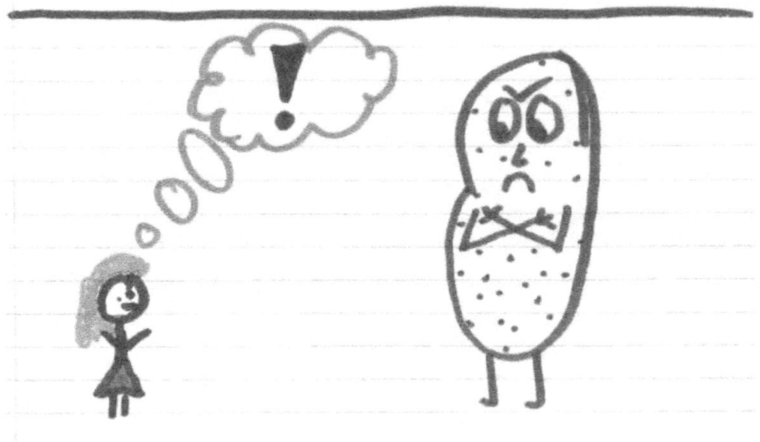

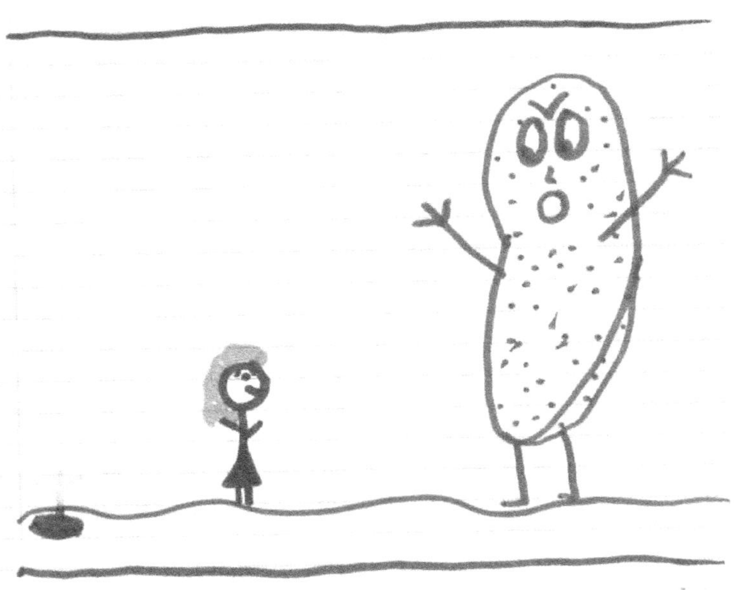

"Listen, small human. I am here to collect all of my brothers," he boomed.

"Who are your brothers?"

"Little brothers in ground." He pointed to the massive potato fields behind her.

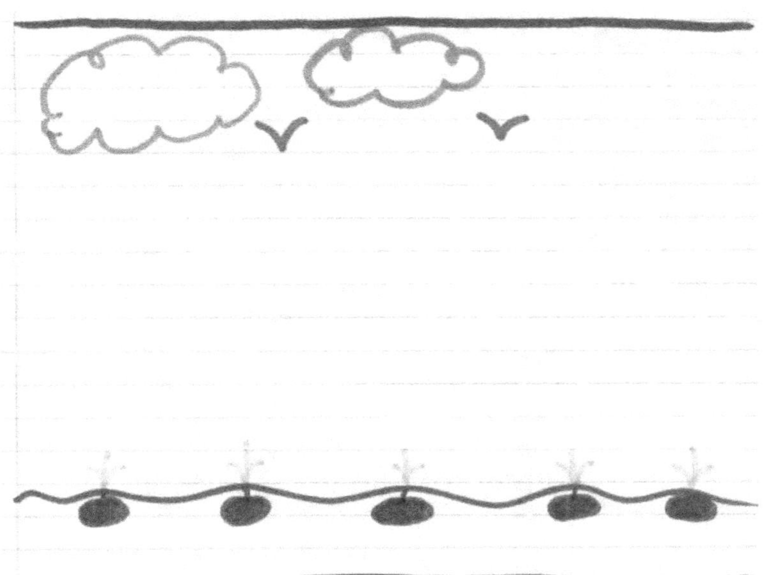

"But they belong to my father," Tina said.

The potato frowned. "NO. My brothers!"

Tina gulped. "But we are still raising them. They're not ready to go yet."

"Nonsense! You fetch them and give them to me!"

"No! These are our potatoes and you can't just take them!"

The potato did not like this.

"I AM SPUDDICUS AND YOU WILL GIVE ME MY BROTHERS, OR I WILL EAT YOU!!"

At that moment, Tina hatched a plan.

"Okay, Spuddicus. I understand. I will go get your brothers."

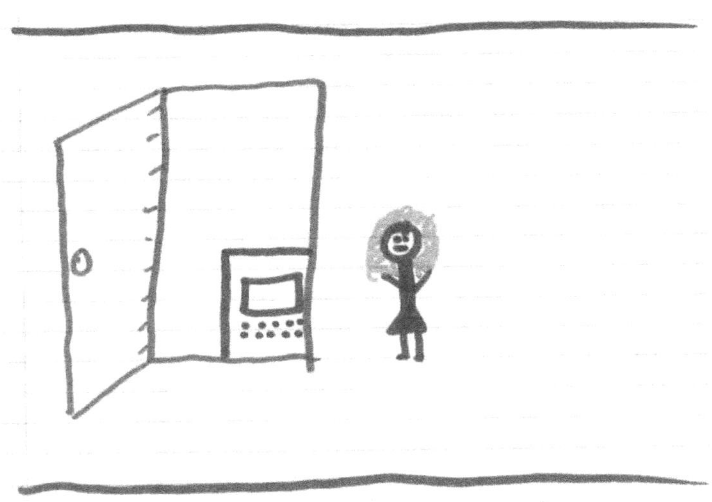

At that, Tina turned to walk to her father's shed, where he kept all their farm tools. She shut the door so Spuddicus couldn't see inside. Then, she opened a secret door in the back that led to a small kitchen.

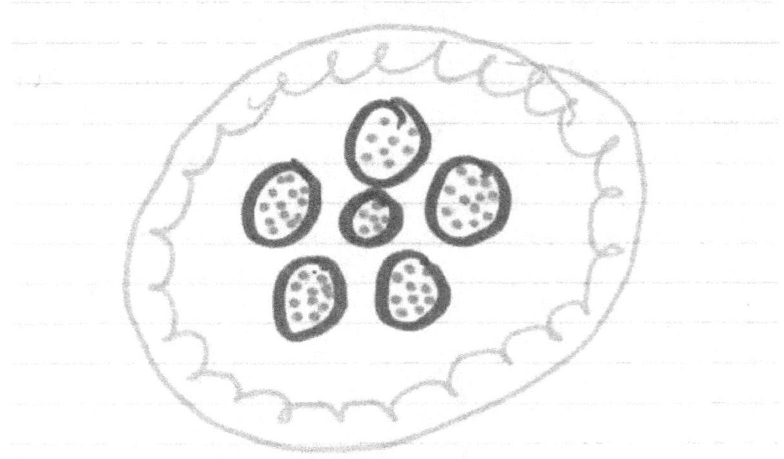

You see, there were special cookies that Tina made that would lull anyone to sleep that ate them. She had made an extra batch the night before, and she thought, “What a perfect way to distract Spuddicus!” So, she took six cookies and she spread them out across her nicest plate.

Once Tina had the cookies, she carefully closed the kitchen door and left the shed to deliver her special treats to Spuddicus.

“This is not my brothers!” Spuddicus stomped his foot. “Give me my brothers!”

“These are just some cookies to snack on while I fetch your brothers. I hope you like them.”

“Thank you, small human.” He took the plate and began munching right away. Tina started back toward the shed to get her tools.

She watched Spuddicus through the window as he fell to the ground and went to sleep. The plan worked! Spuddicus was fast asleep, and when Tina walked up to him and nudged him, but he didn’t stir.

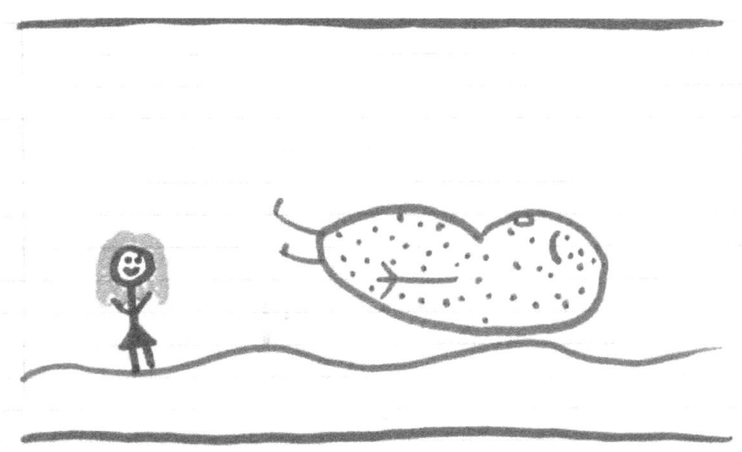

"Father! Come look! A giant potato!"

Tina's father came running, and when he saw it, he was proud.

Then they both hatched the same idea.

"Let's roll him away so he doesn't find us again," said Tina.

And that is exactly what they did. They rolled him to the nearest giant potato community, and Spuddicus lived there happily the rest of his days.

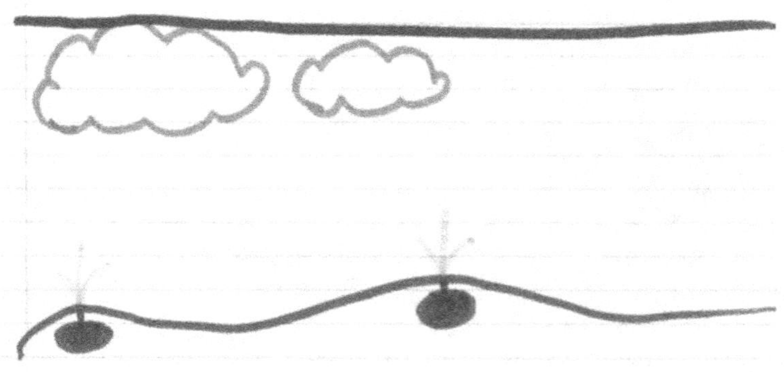

THE END

The Book of King Collin

David Bodnar, Justin Caleb Lee, Robert Varner

In all the land, King Collin, the lion, was loved by all. Everyone thought he was a great king. To feed the kingdom, King Collin gave out chocolate bars to every single animal.

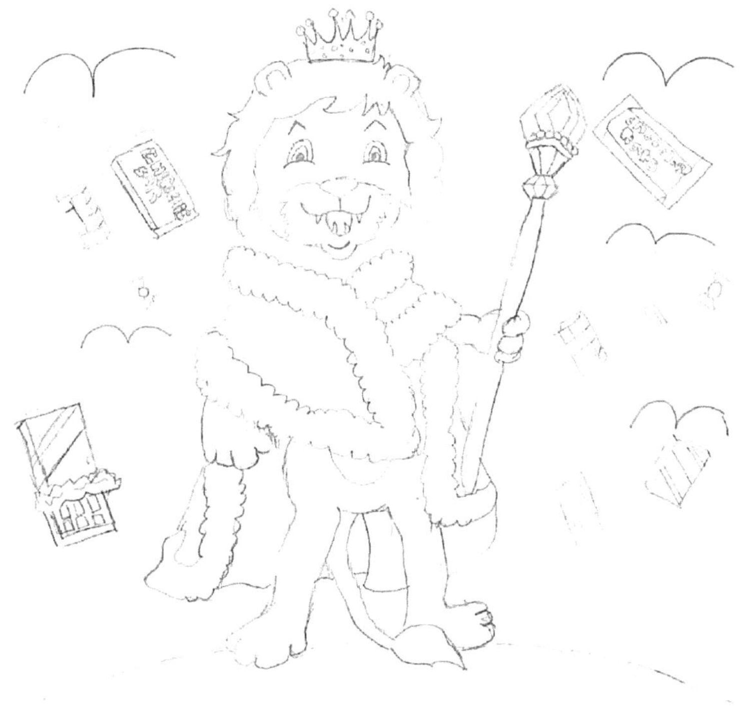

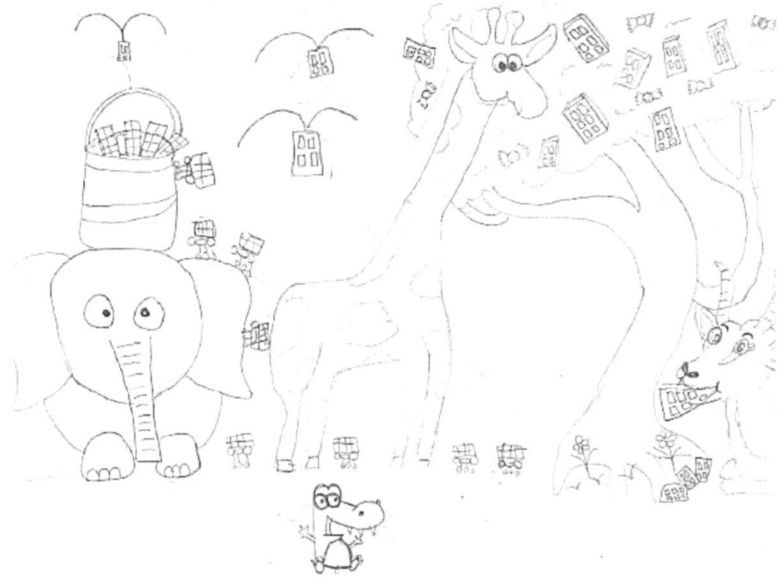

The amazing antelope picked all the low chocolate for all the Land. All the really tall Giraffes picked all the really high hard-to-reach chocolate bars.

The many awesome ants picked up and carried chocolate bars to the storage house. Then the big strong elephants carried them on to be dropped by the birds. The great gorillas were the mighty knights guarding the land.

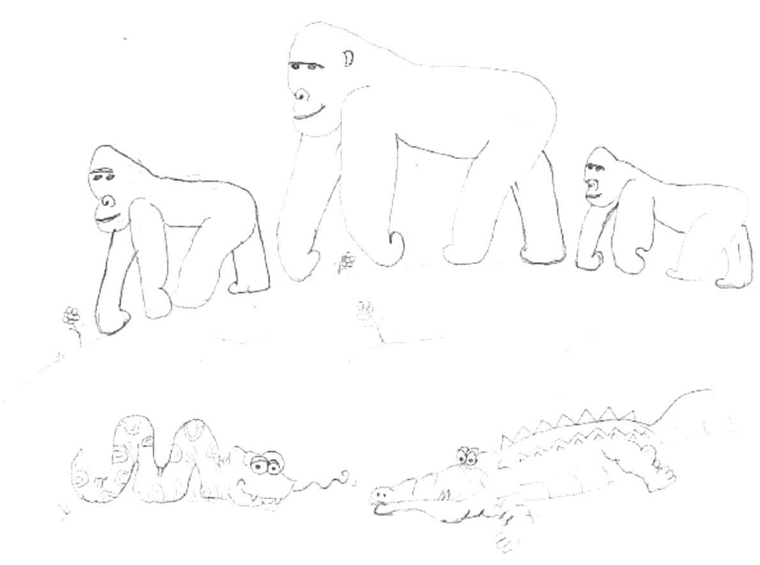

Until, one day there was a shortage of chocolate bars. King Collin noticed that the snakes, lizards, and alligators were being lazy and not helping the kingdom. He decided that the snakes, lizards, and alligators weren't allowed any more chocolate bars.

This made the laziest, meanest, nastiest, foulest, ugliest guy, Andy the anaconda, really really mad. So the evil snake began to talk to all the other lazy reptiles. He told them that King Collin was mean and if they united, they could defeat the mean King, and steal all the chocolate.

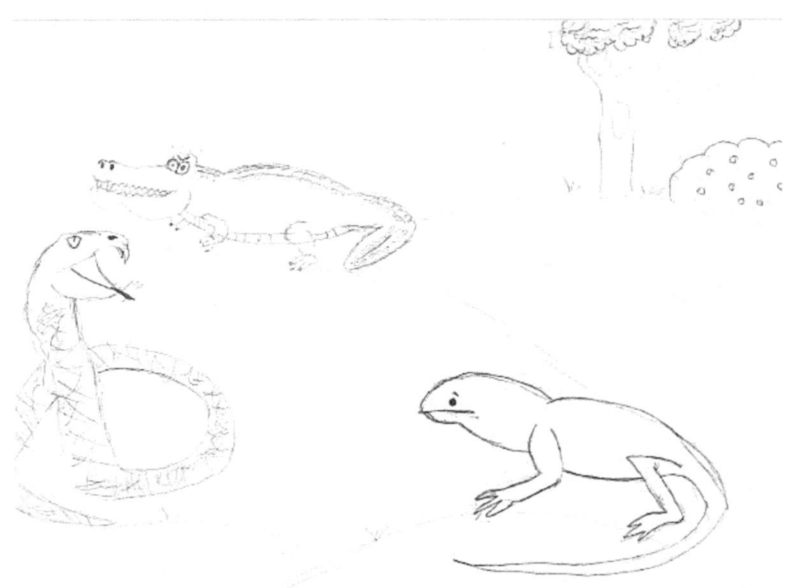

So evil Andy, the big bad beast, makes slimy Stoke the snake, Landon the lying lizard, and Alvin the awful alligator, leaders to create an evil, bad, and no good army. They wanted to defeat King Collin and his forces to get all the chocolate bars for themselves and to take over the animal kingdom.

When King Collin heard about this betrayal, he ordered Jimmie the Gorilla and all the Great Gorillas Knights to defend King Collin's castle.

When all the snakes, lizards, and alligators saw the Gorillas and how big, brave, strong, and tough the Knights defending the castle were, they became afraid. However, a few spirited snakes, loyal lizards, and audacious alligators still charged the castle.

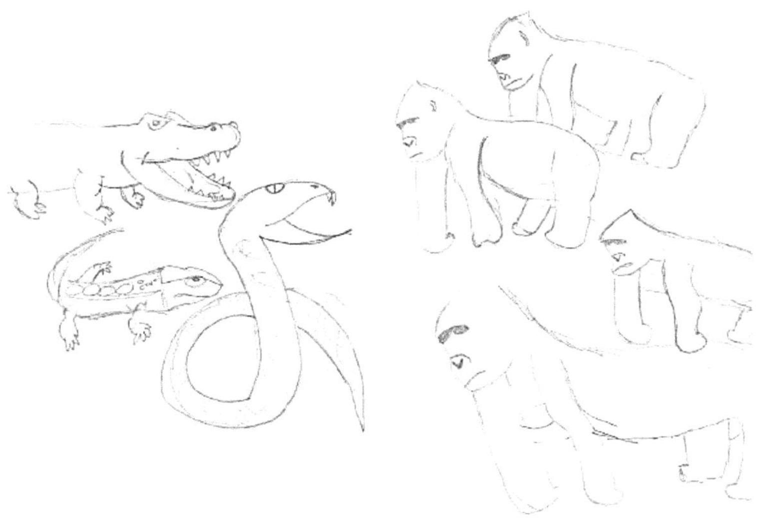

However, Jimmie and all the gorillas stopped the snakes, lizards, and alligators. They also captured Andy, bringing peace to all the land.

Wise King Collin, seeing his army's success, punished Awful Andy to a thousand years in the dungeon. While telling all the reptiles that if they just planted more chocolate trees there would be no more shortages of chocolate and everyone would have enough to eat.

The reptiles listened to what King Collin said. And all the other animals did their best to help the kingdom as usual. The animal king had peace and joy for one thousand years and they lived happily ever after.

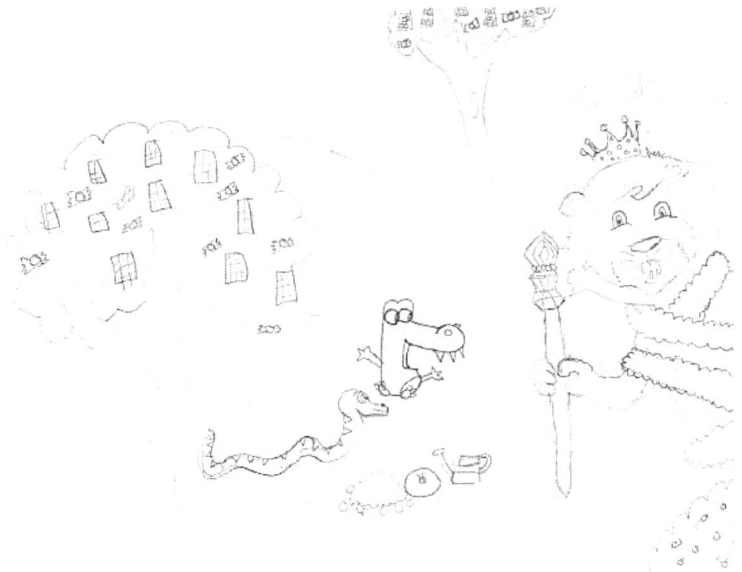

Super Girl

Hannah Calfee and Alexia Thompson

Once upon a time there was a big beautiful castle that sat up on a hill that overlooked the rest of the kingdom.

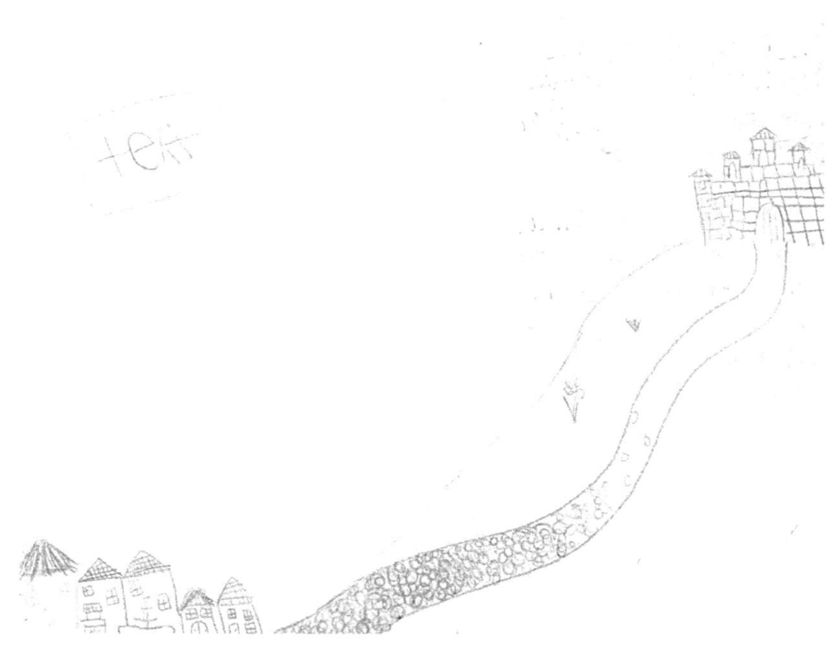

This was a very special day for the kingdom. King Jacob was about to crown one of his sons, Prince Nicholas, the new king. King Jacob had another son Prince Caleb.

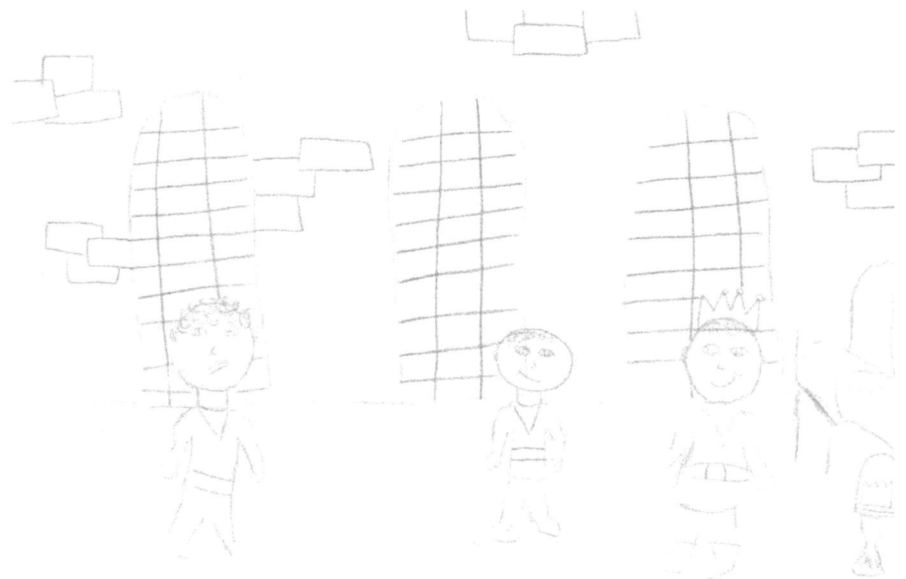

When Caleb found out he wasn't going to be king he got very jealous. In a fit of rage, Caleb wished that Nicholas would be taken away, so he could be the king instead.

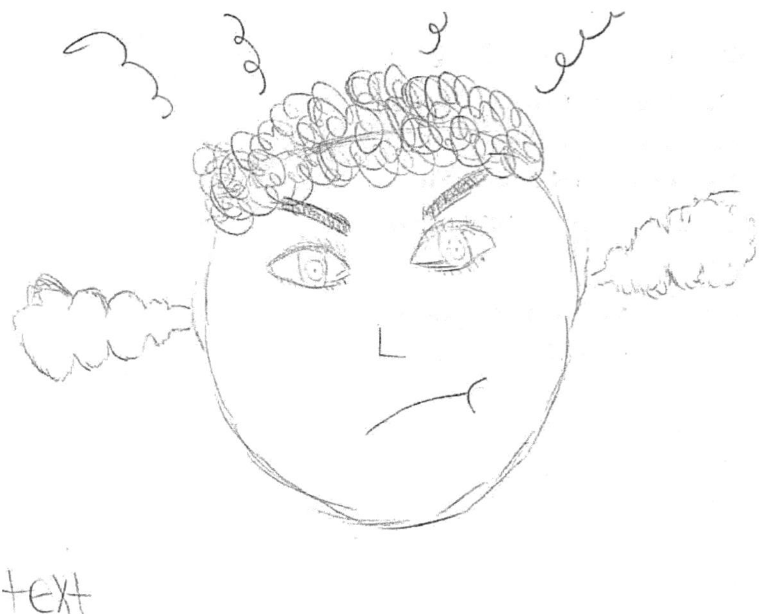

He did not realize what he had done, but an evil witch who lived outside the kingdom heard his wish. So that night while Prince Nicholas was sleeping, the witch snuck into the castle and kidnapped him.

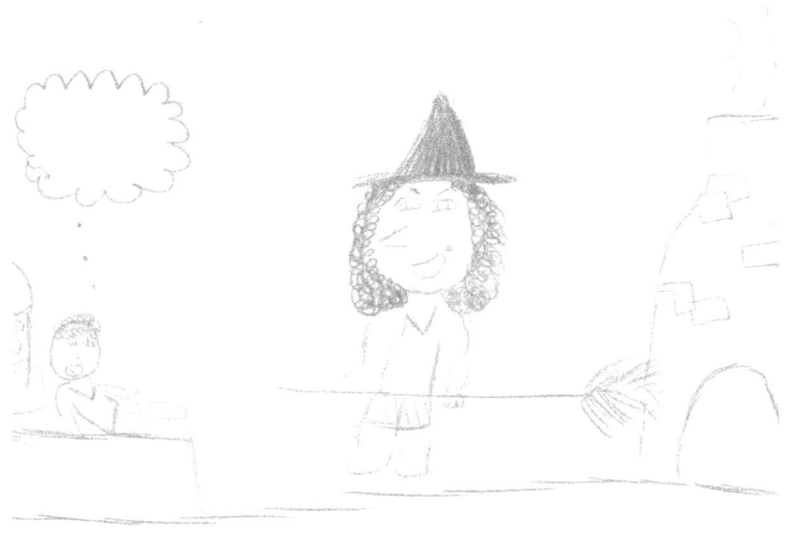

The witch took him to a faraway tower guarded by a big scary dragon where no one could ever find him.

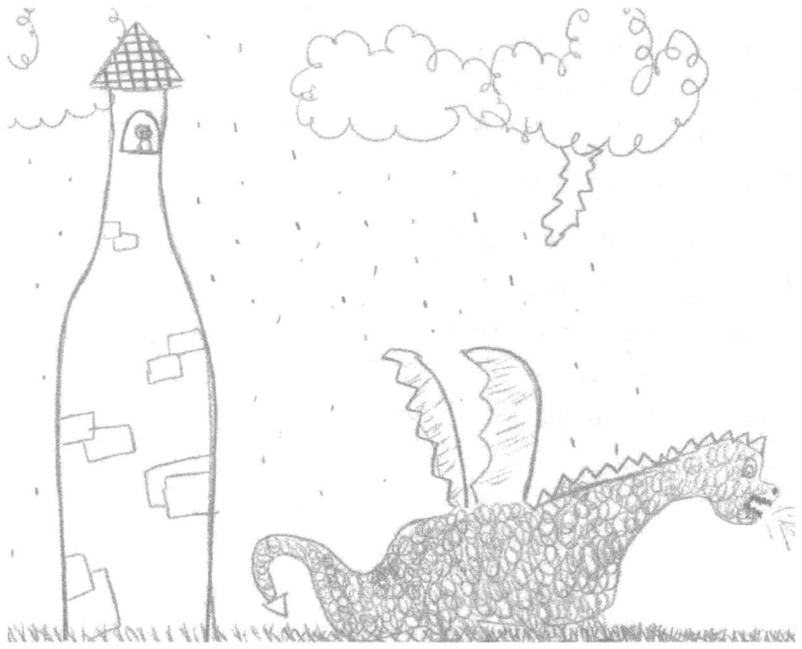

Luckily for Prince Nicholas, the kingdom had a secret hero. There was a very special village girl who lived in the kingdom. Her name was Super girl, and she was the kingdom's superhero. Super girl used her special mind powers to figure out where Prince Nicholas was.

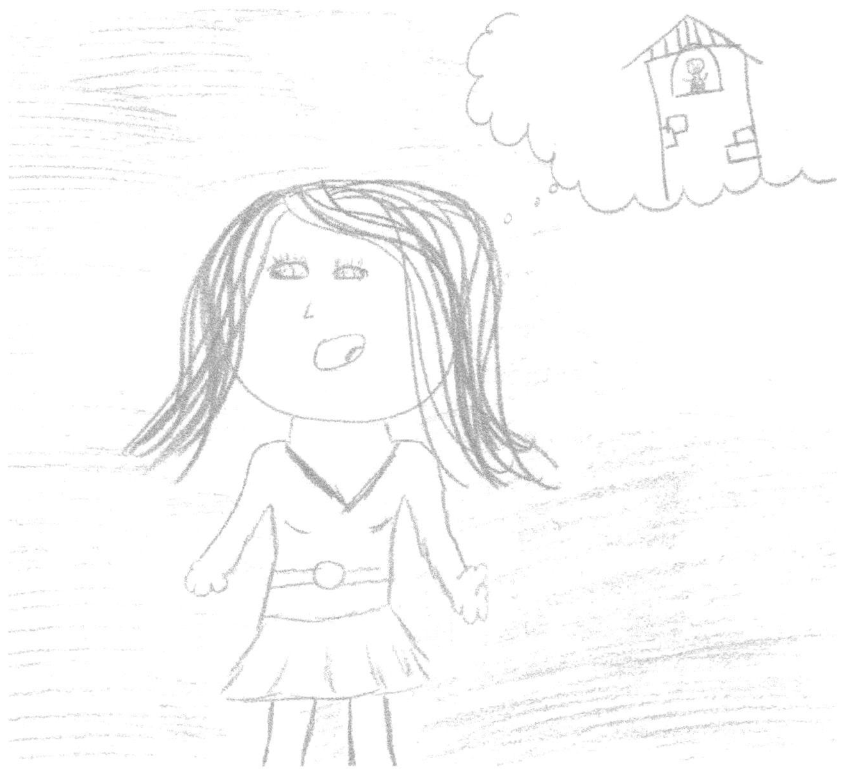

After a long journey of flying, she reached the mysterious tower where the witch hid Prince Nicholas.

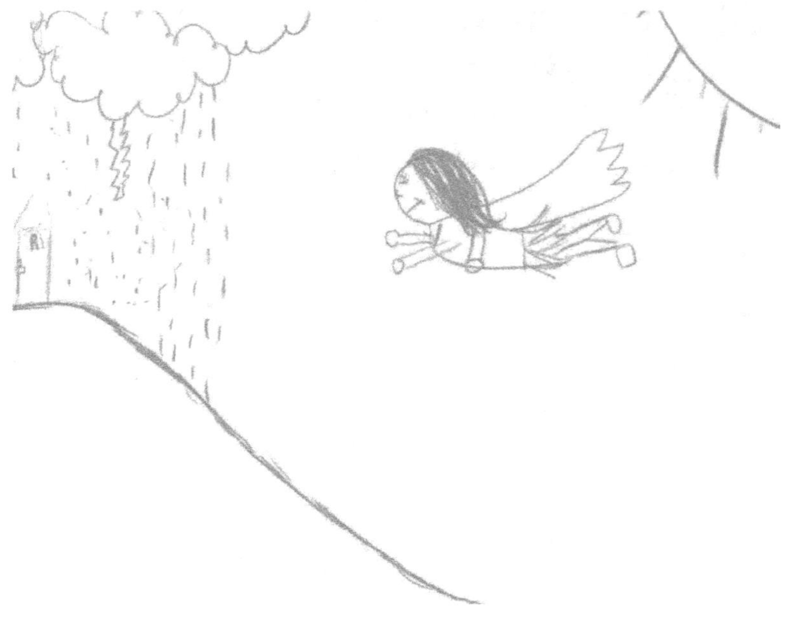

As soon as Super girl got to the tower, the witch appeared and tried to cast a spell on Super girl. But Super girl was prepared. She used her secret freeze gun to stop the witch and the dragon, so she could sneak into the tower.

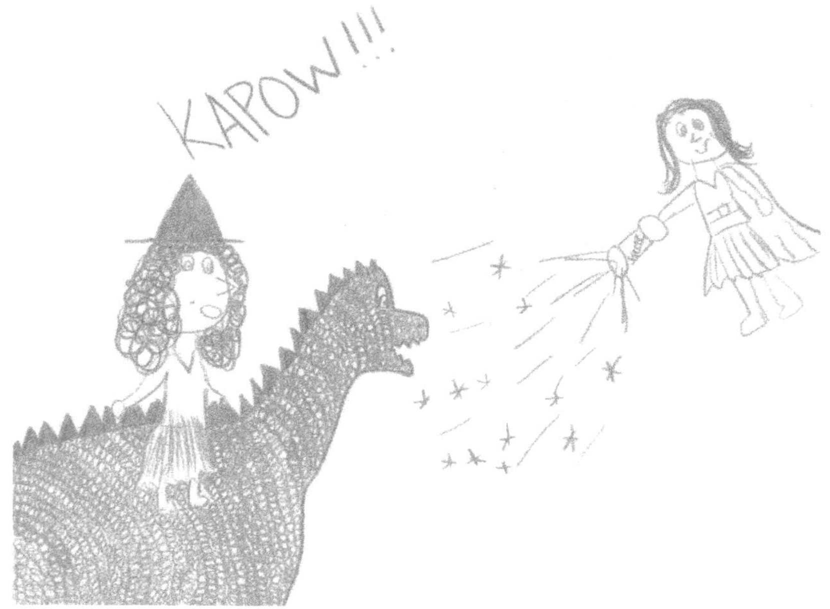

Super girl got to the tower and rescued the Prince Nicholas. Super girl took Prince Nicholas back home to the castle, and they told King Jacob what had happened.

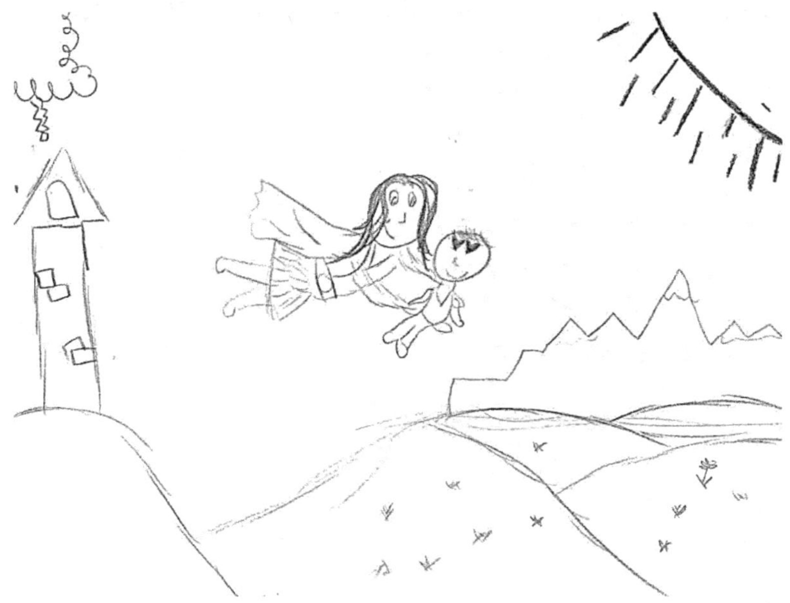

The King Jacob was very mad, so he put the Prince Caleb in jail, so he couldn't harm anyone else.

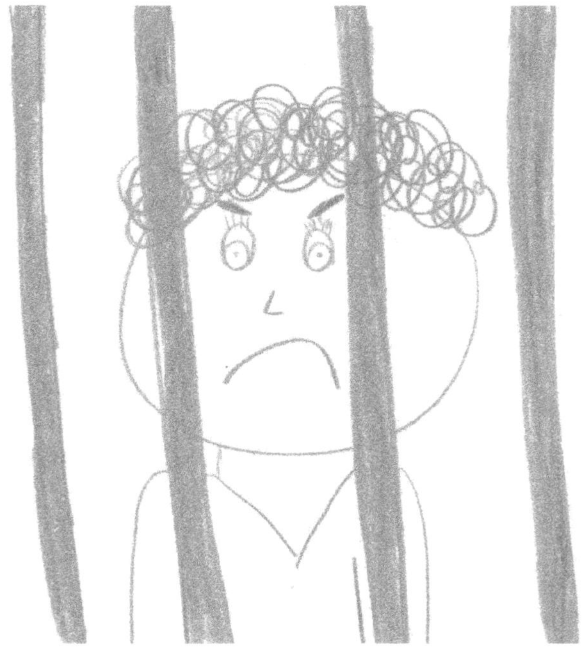

Prince Nicholas was so happy to be home, and he was so grateful for Super girl that he asked her to marry him. So Prince Nicholas became King Nicholas, and he married Super girl and they lived happily ever after.

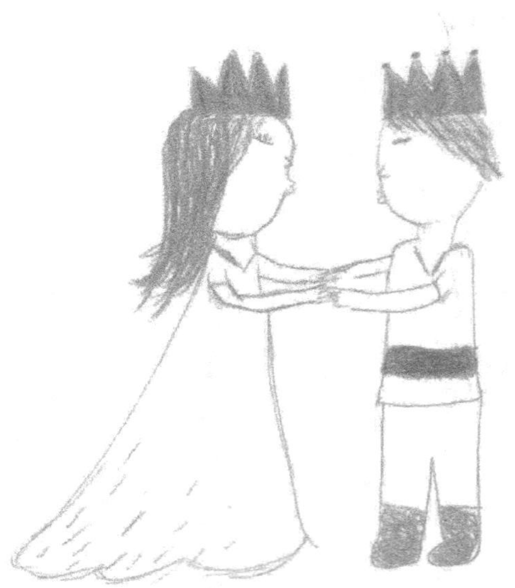

How to Take Care of a Dog

Addysonn Shugars

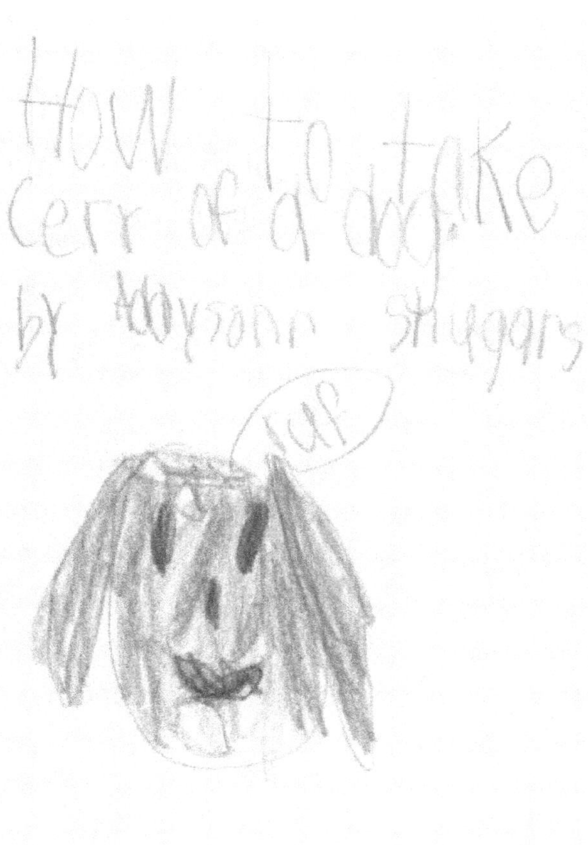

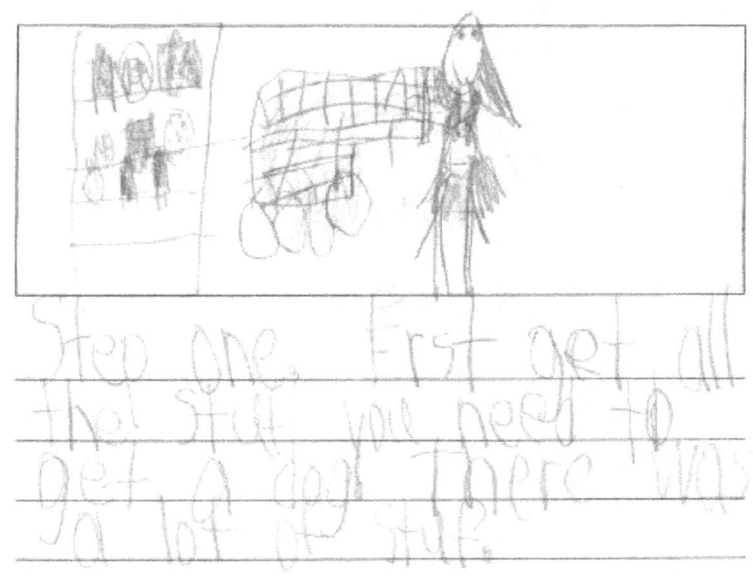

Step One: First get all the stuff you need to get a dog. There was a lot of stuff.

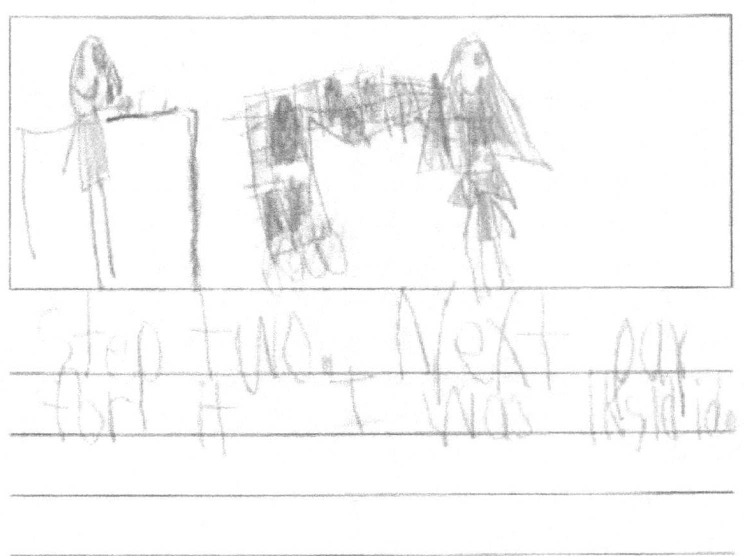

Step Two: Next pay for it. I was excited.

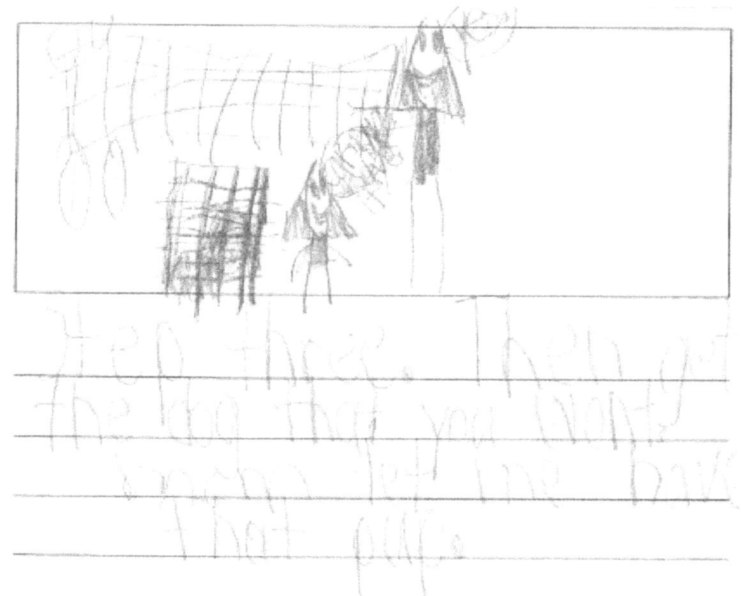

Step Three: Then get the dog that you want. Mom let me have that pup.

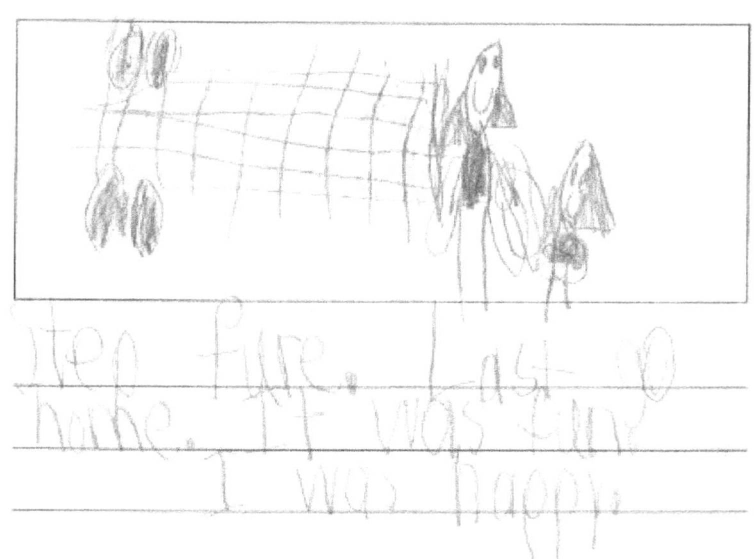

Step Four: Last, go home. It was fun. I was happy.

The Time I Busted My Chin

Andrina Cooper

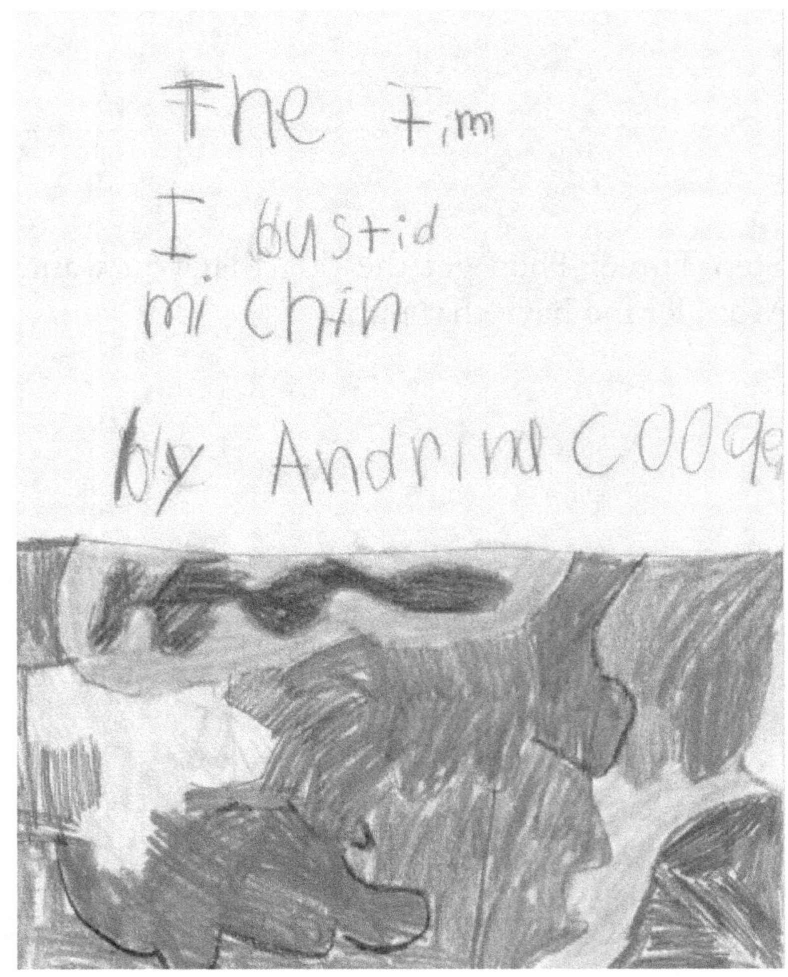

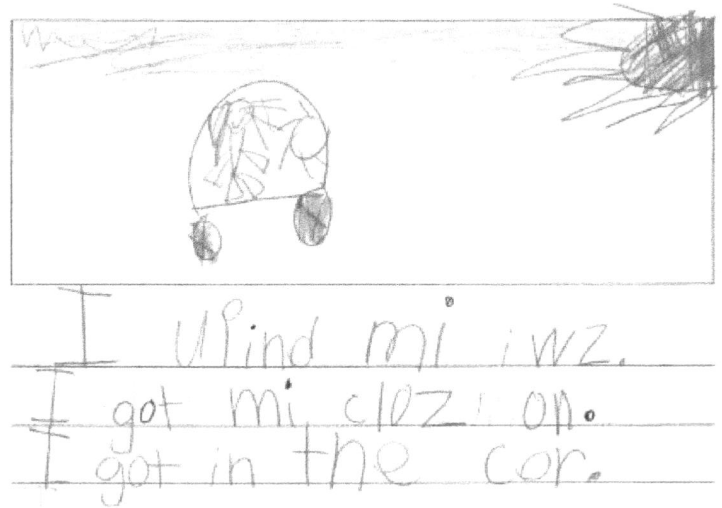

I opened my eyes. I got my clothes on. I got in the car.

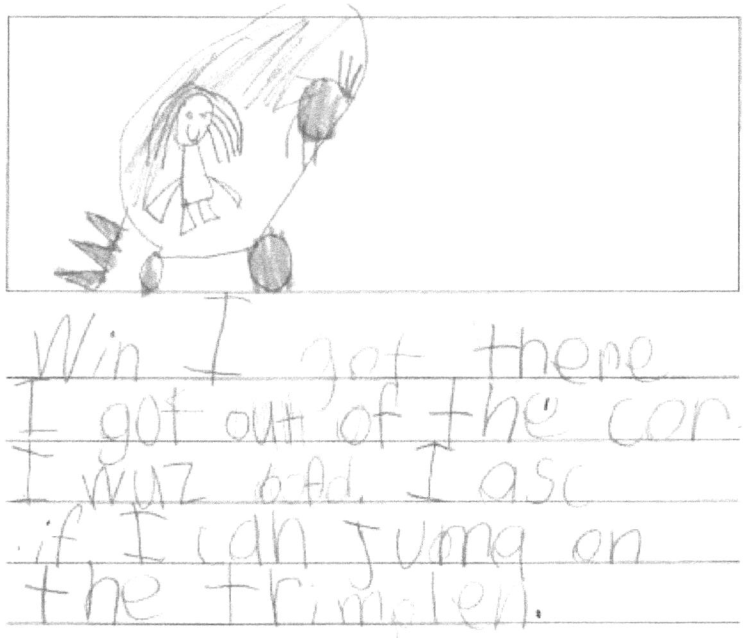

When I got there I got out of the car. I was bored. I asked if I can jump on the trampoline.

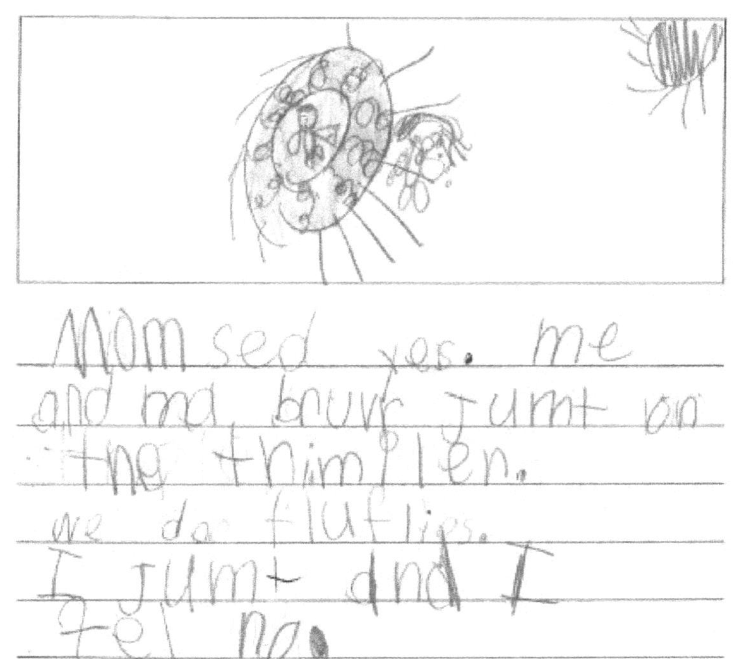

Mom said yes. Me and my brother jumped on the trampoline. We did flip flops. I jumped and I fell no.

I Hope the Seed Grows

Ashby Miller

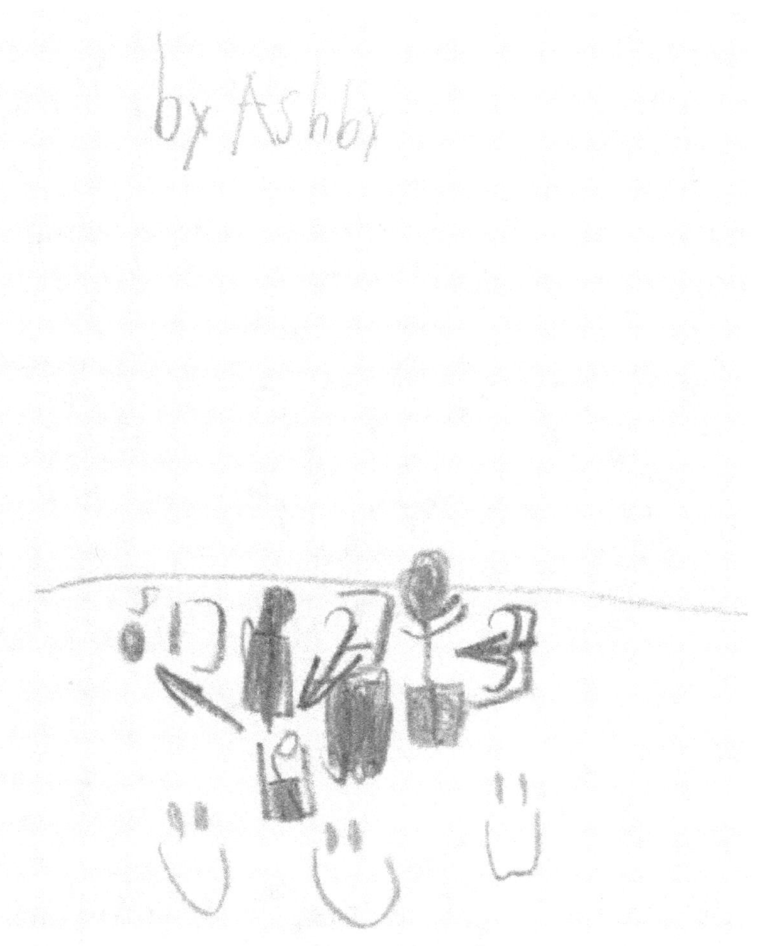

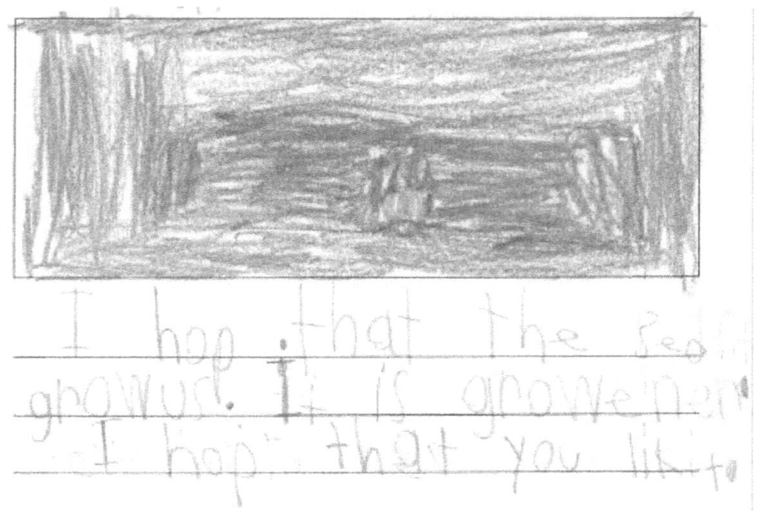

I hope that the seed grows. It is growing. I hope that you like it.

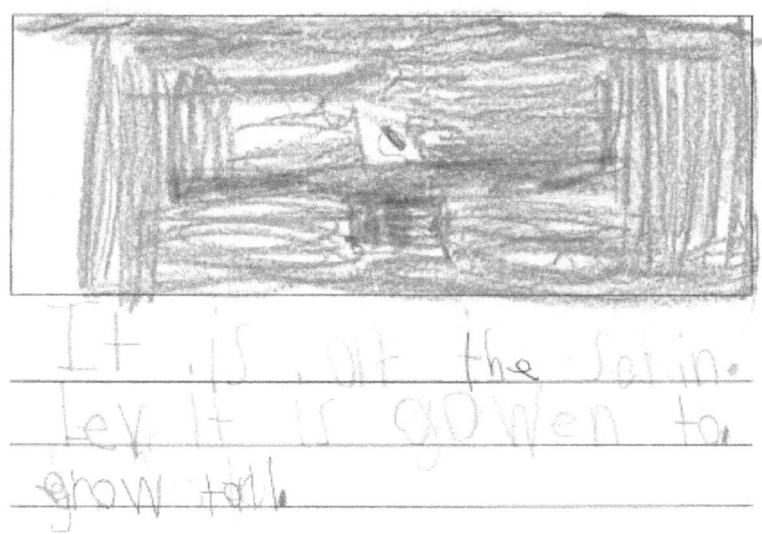

It is outside. Leave it. It is going to grow tall.

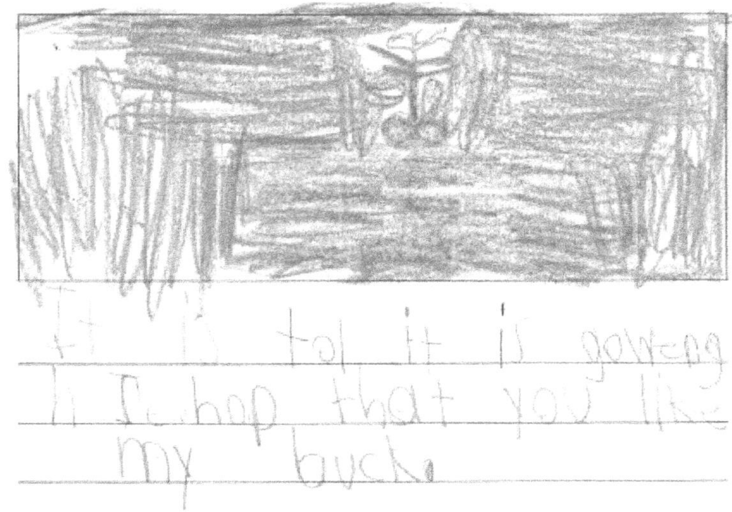

It is tall. It is growing. I hope that you like my book.

I Fell Off My Bed at Night

Landon Whitaker

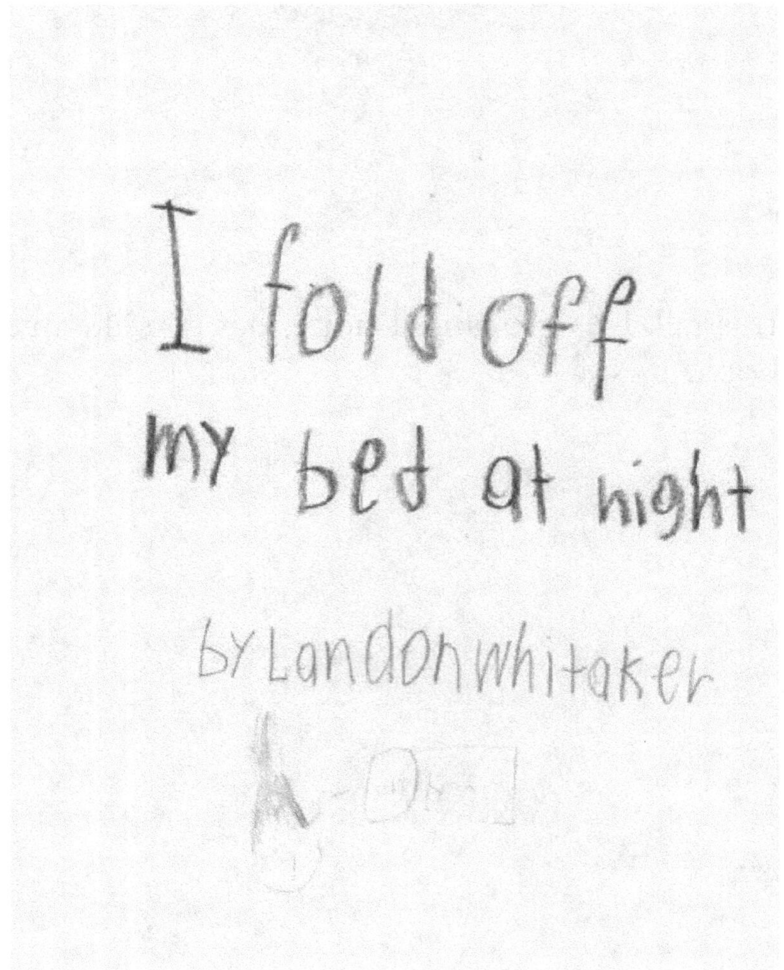

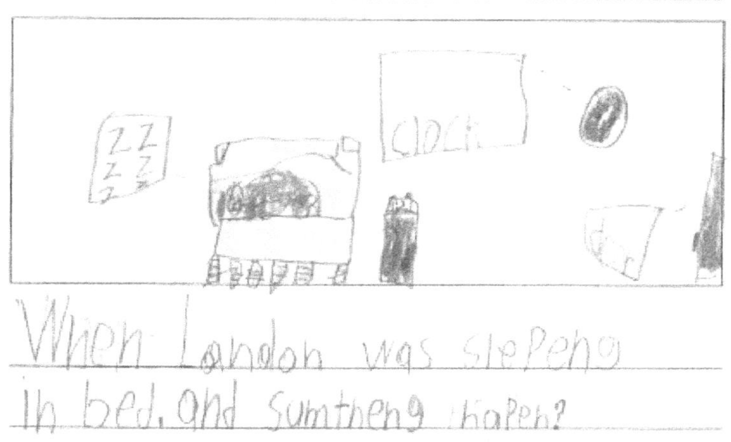

When Landon was sleeping in bed. And something happened?

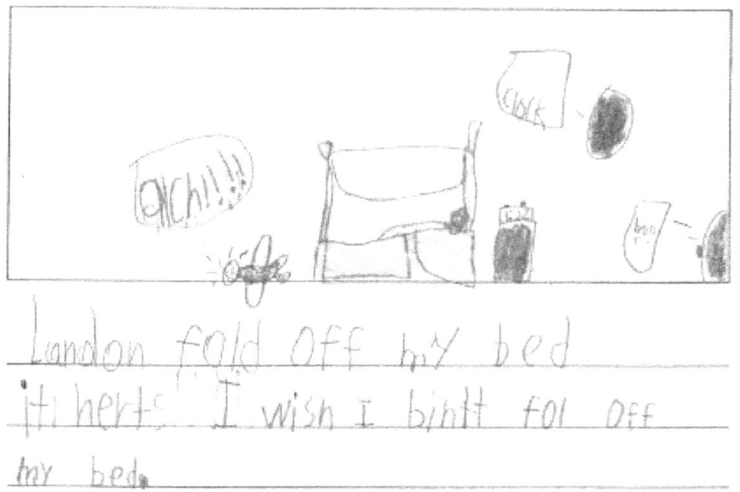

Landon fell off my bed. It hurts! I wish I didn't fall off my bed.

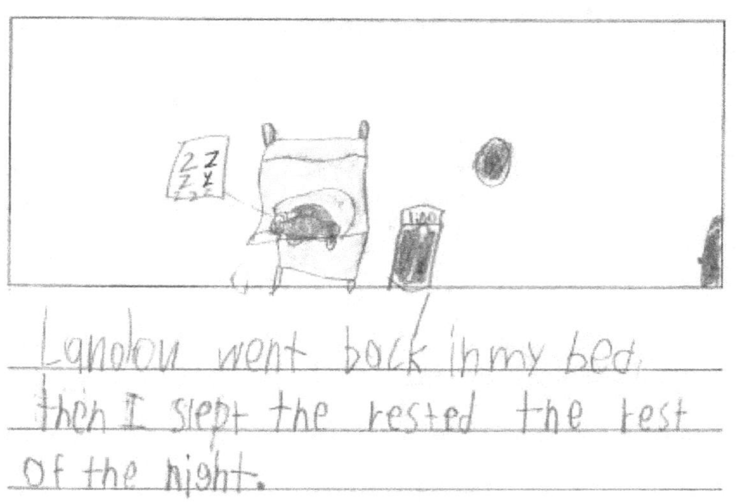

Landon went back in my bed then I slept the rest of the night.

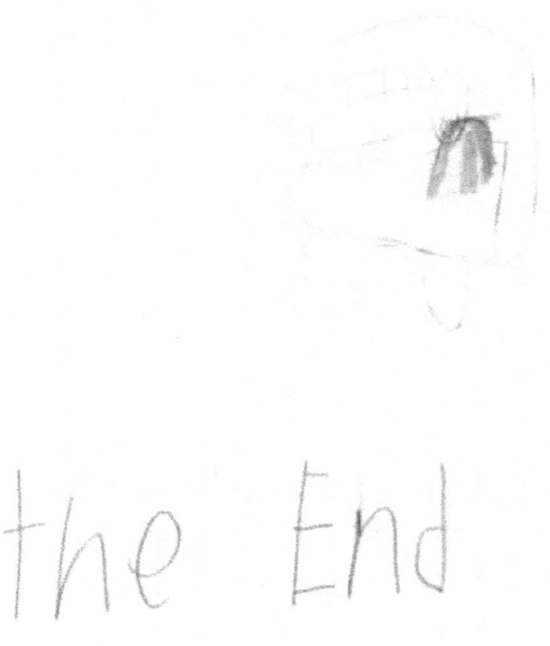

The Day at Disneyworld

Caleb Mallick

The day at Disnewrld.

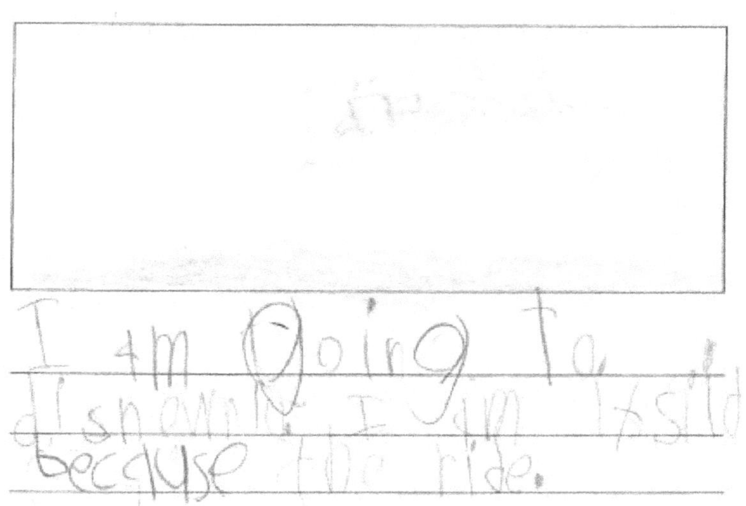

I am going to Disneyworld. I am excited because of the ride.

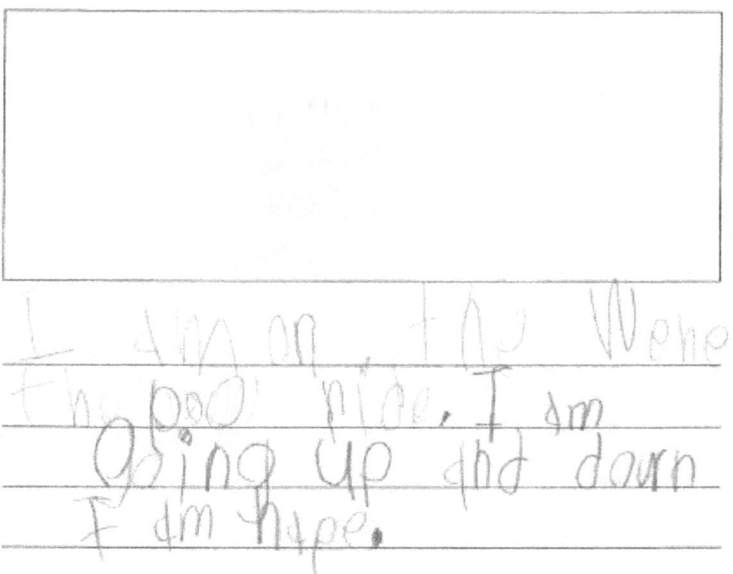

I am on the Winnie the Pooh ride. I am going up and down. I am happy.

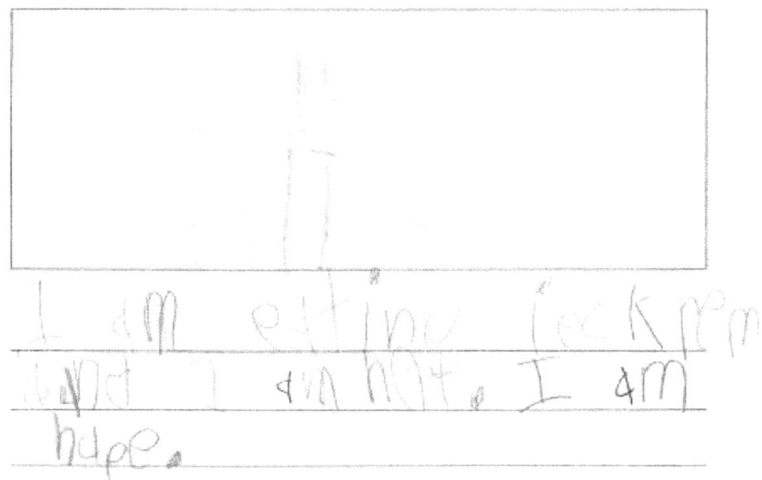

I am eating ice cream and I am hot. I am happy.

Wrestling

Camren Gyurnek

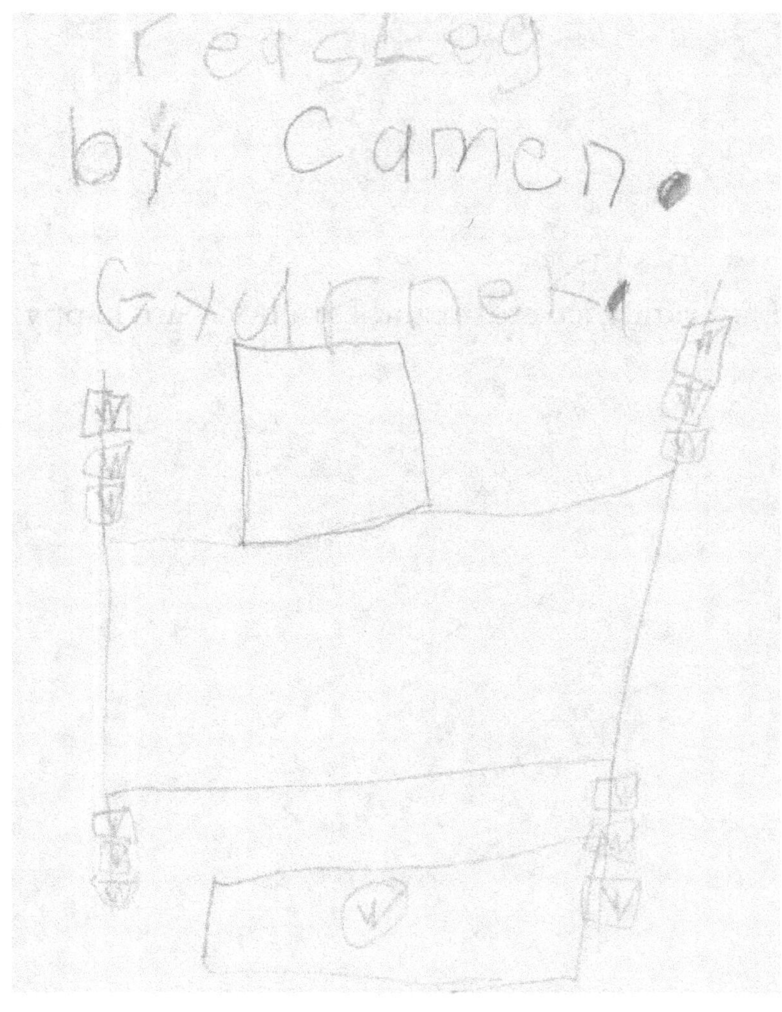

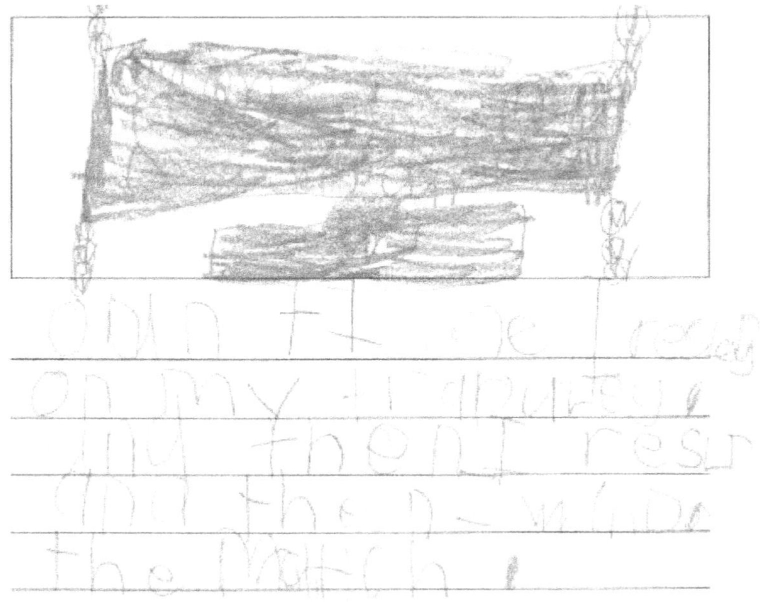

One time I wrestled on my trampoline. And then I wrestled and then I win the match.

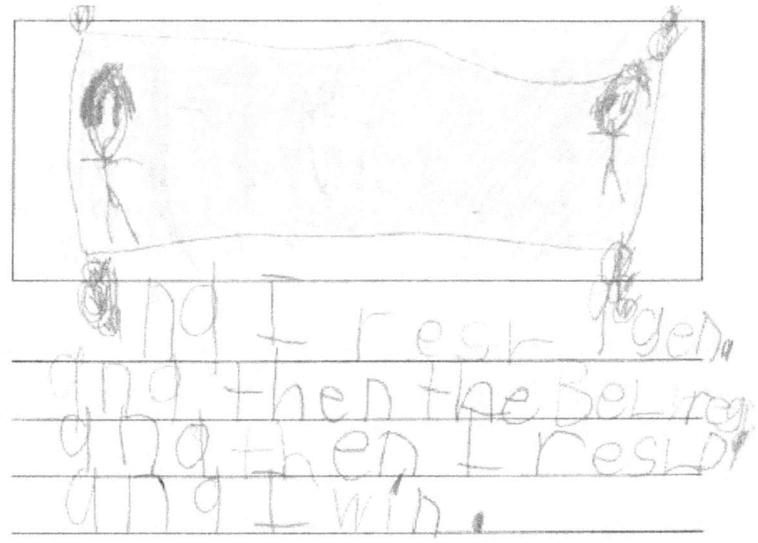

And I wrestled again. And then the bell rang. And then I wrestled and I win.

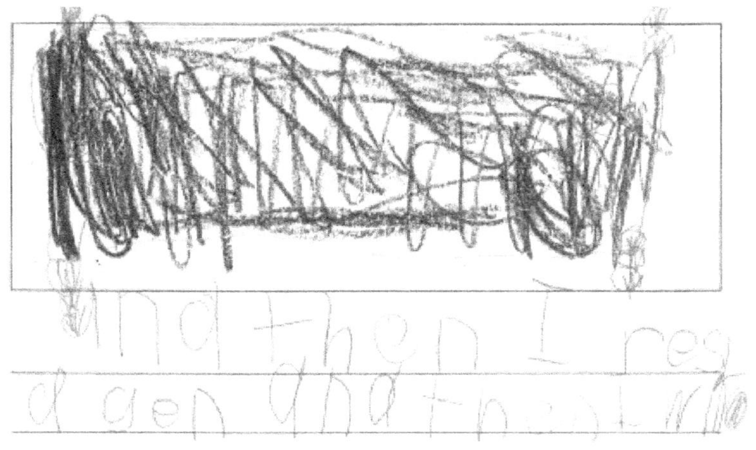

And then I wrestled again and then I win.

This Book is Made by Clinton Nobles

Clinton Nobles

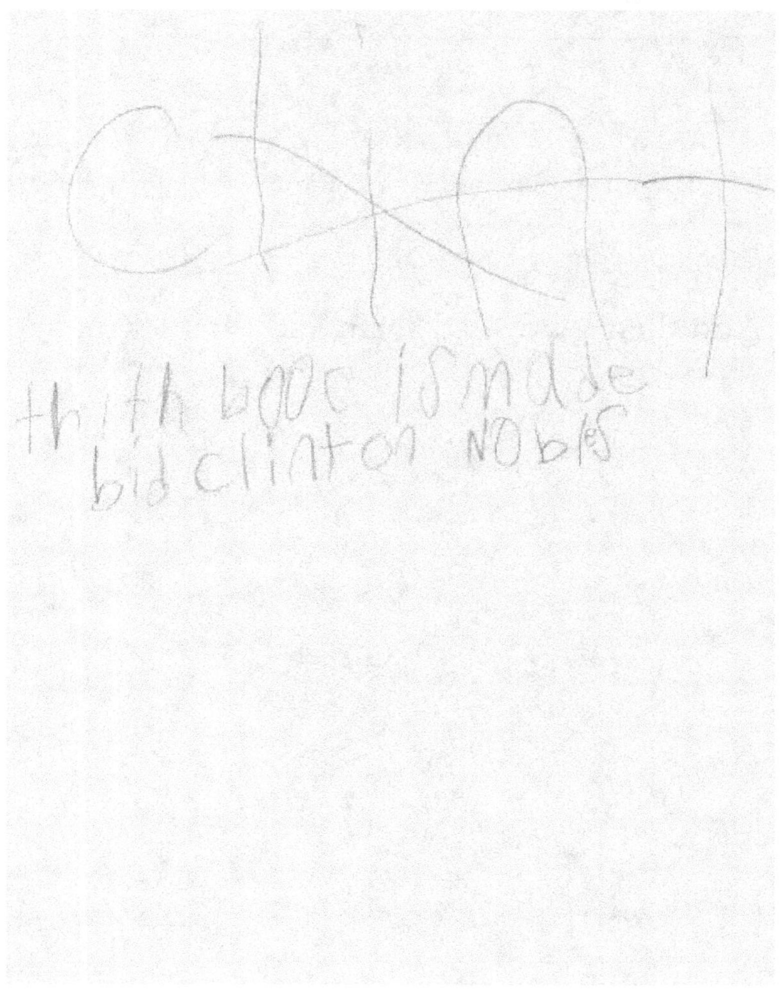

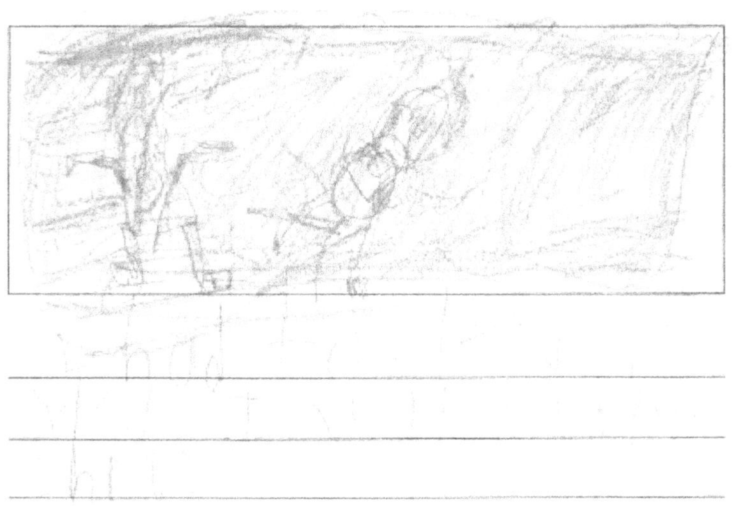

I had to leave my school. I went on the train.

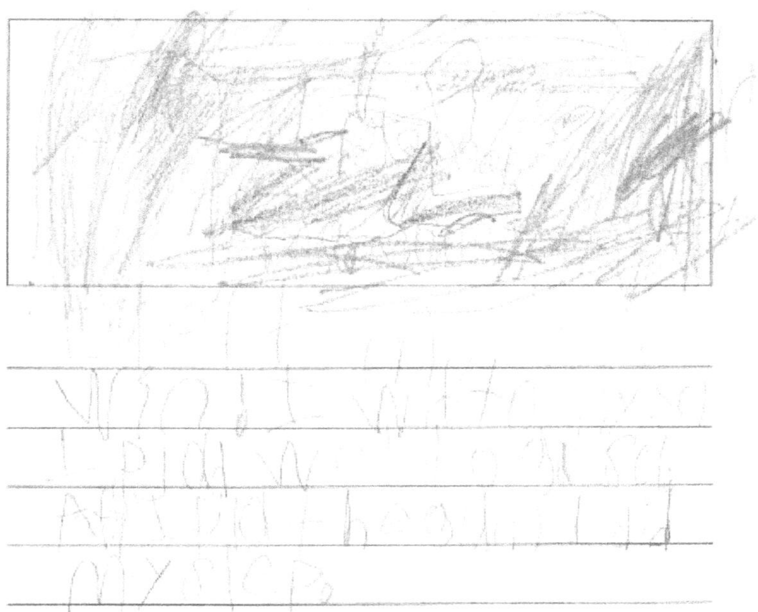

I left my school. When I went to my school I played. Went to grade school. After I played the game I did my sleep.

We stopped at Baskin Robbin's when I slept. I slept again.

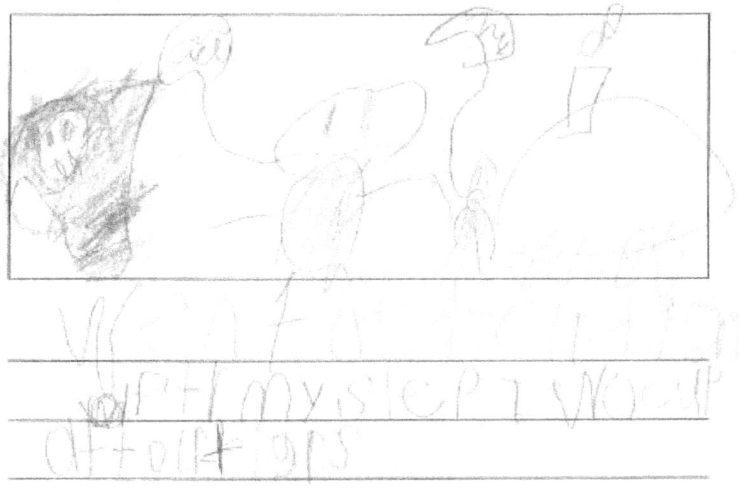

Went to their tigers. After my sleep I woke up at Taylor Tigers.

clint

Getting My First Cat

Emily Hall

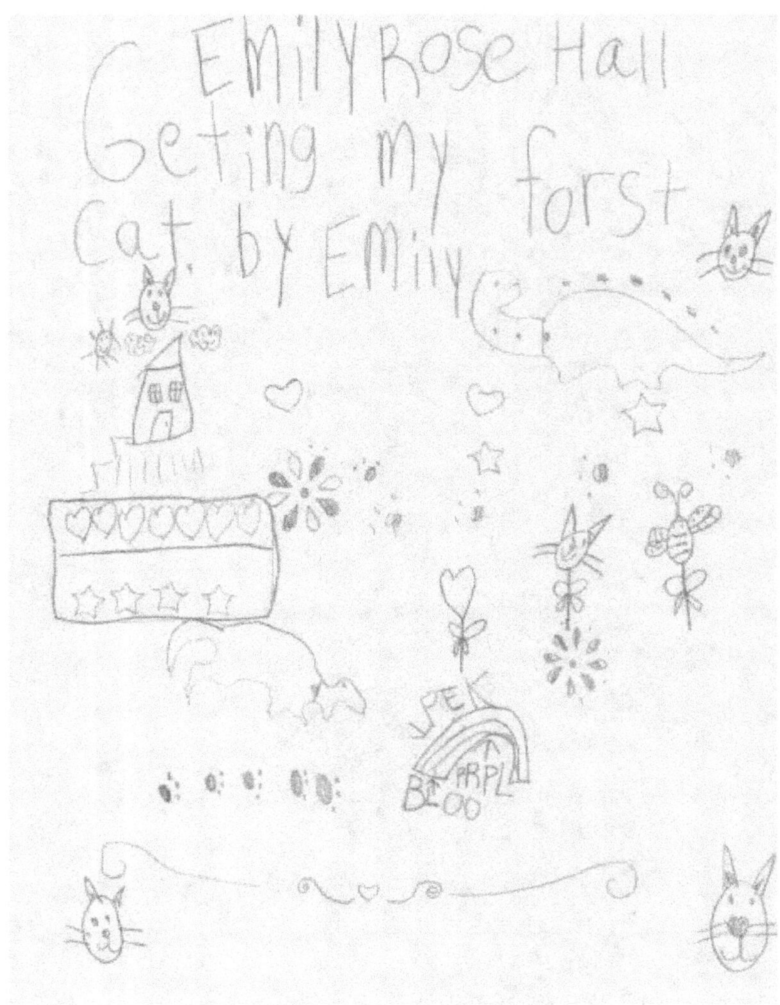

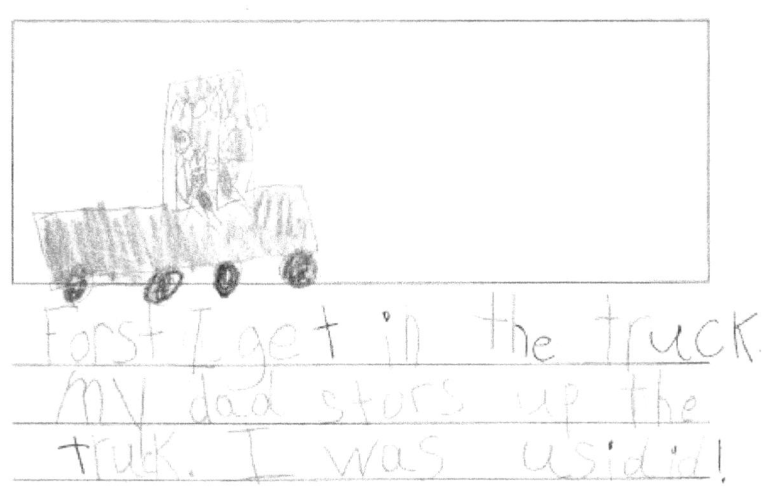

First I get in the truck. My dad starts up the truck. I was excited!

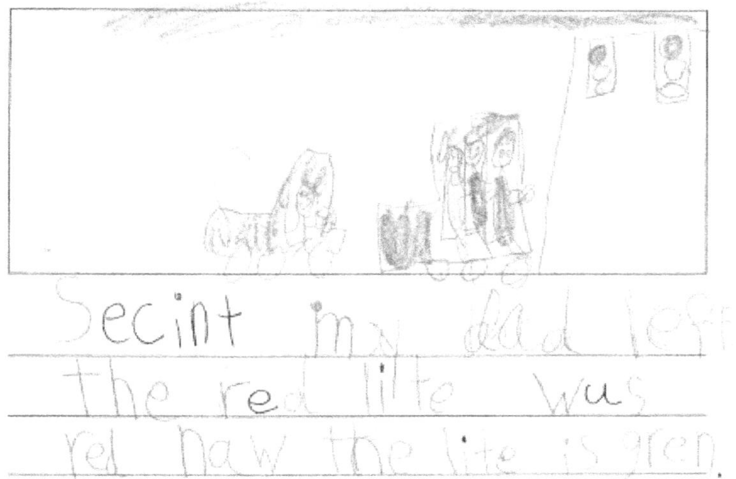

The second my dad left the red light was red, now the light is green.

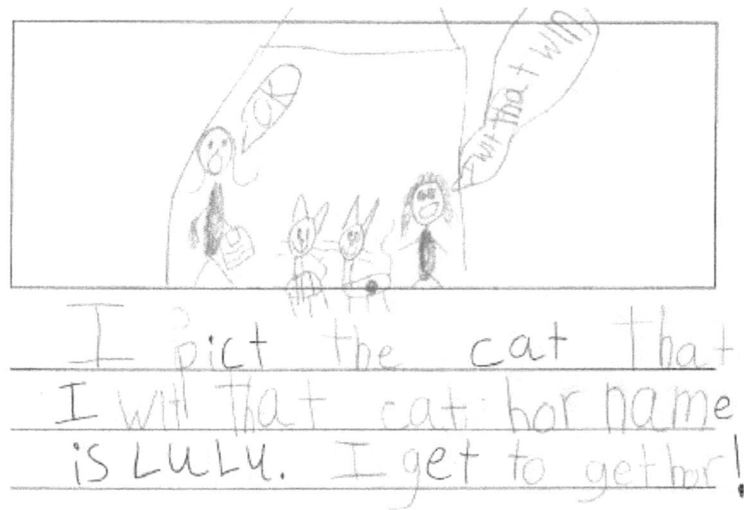

I picked the cat that I want. That cat. Her name is Lulu. I get to get her!

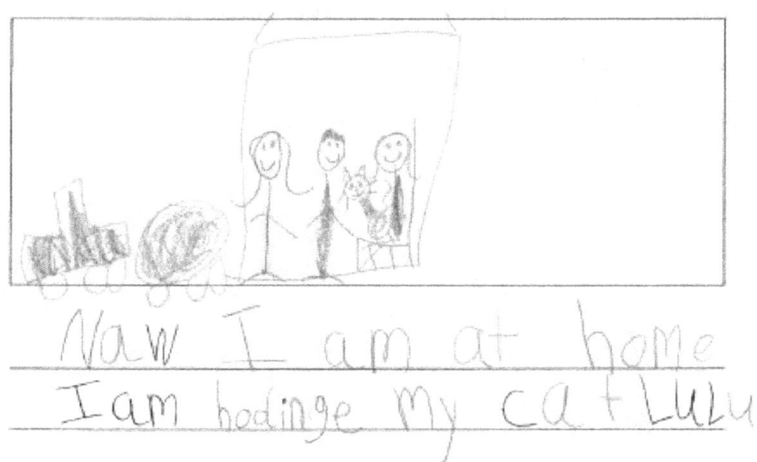

Now I am at home. I am holding my cat Lulu.

I Went to Pick Up My Cousin

Emily Casler

I went to go Pick up my cusin.
by Emily C

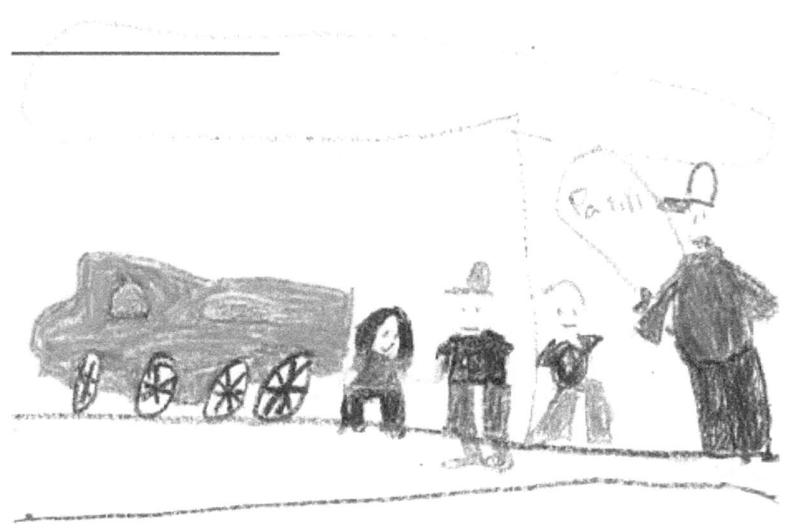

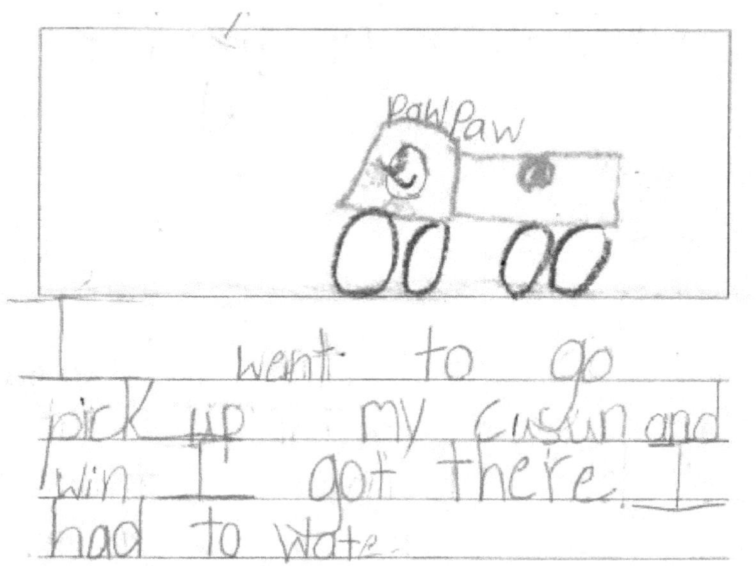

I went to go pick up my cousin and when I got there I had to wait.

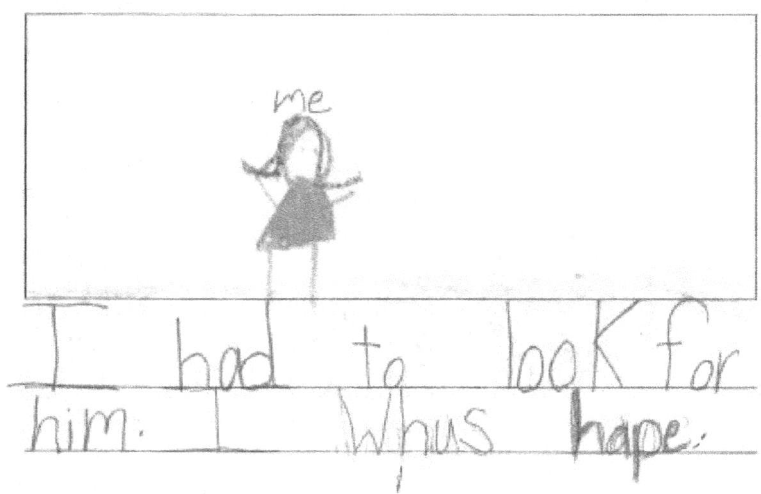

I had to look for him. I was happy.

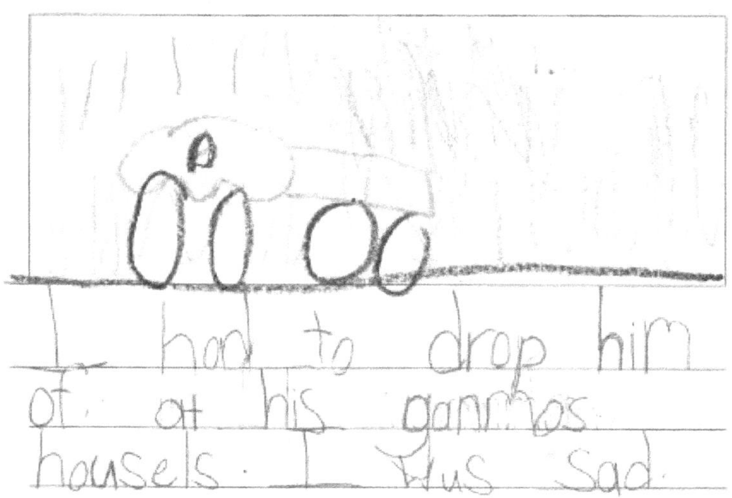

I had to drop him off at his grandma's house.
I was sad.

Dirt Bike Championship

Henley Hager

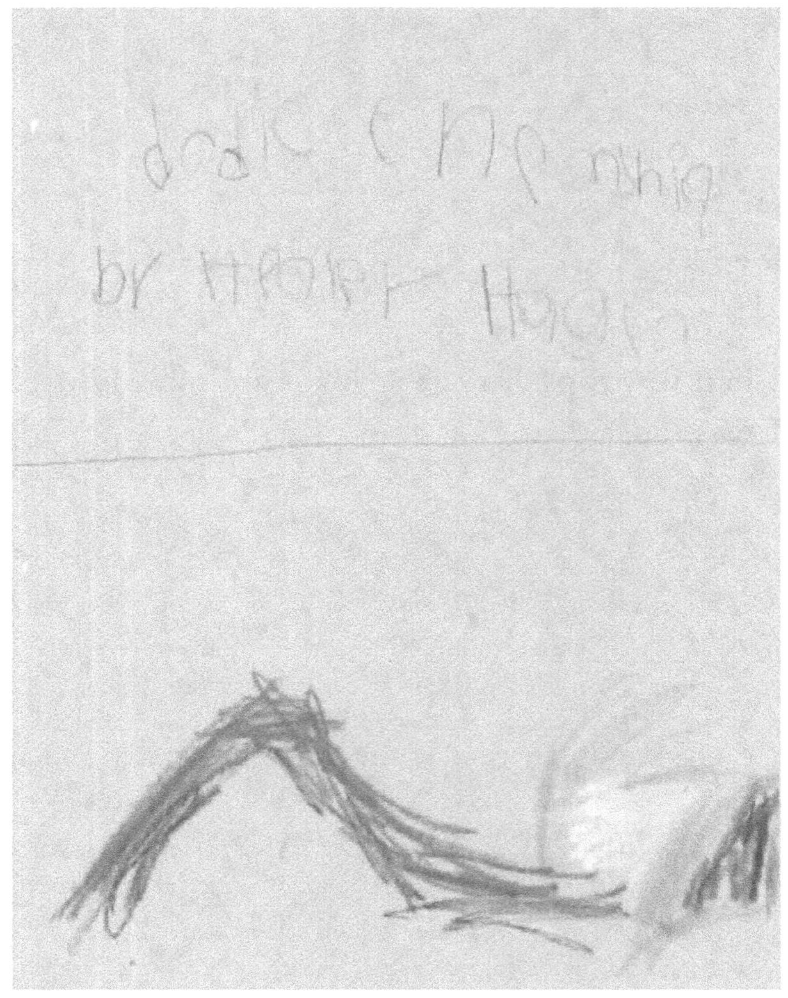

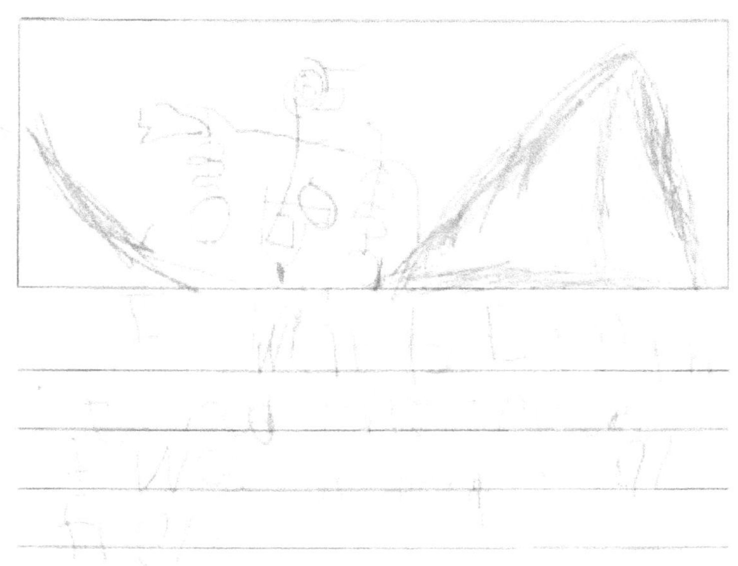

I went to exgames. I rode the track. I was scared at first.

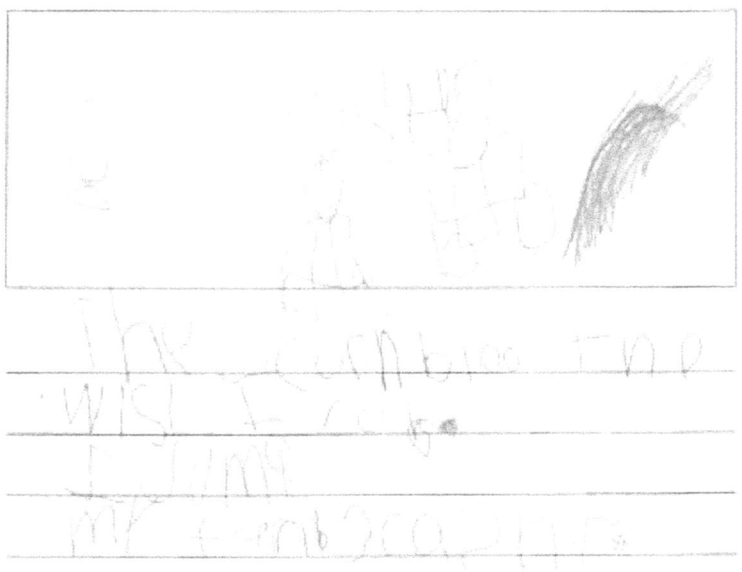

The coach blew the whistle. I rode. I jumped. My friend crashed.

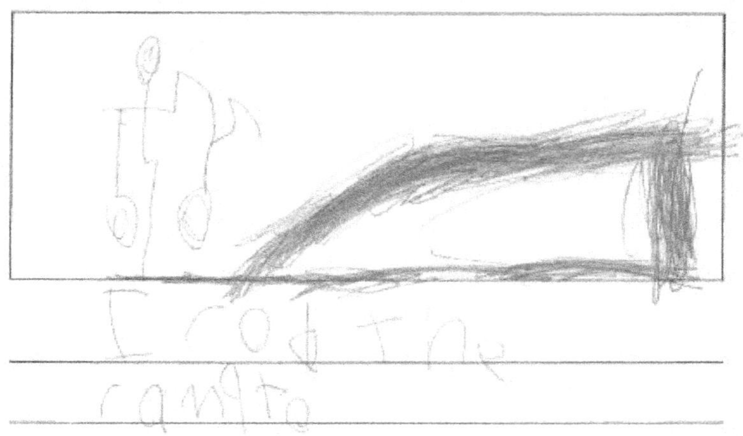

I rode the ramp.

The Lockdown Drill

Hunter Harvey

The lock down drill

by Hunter Harvey

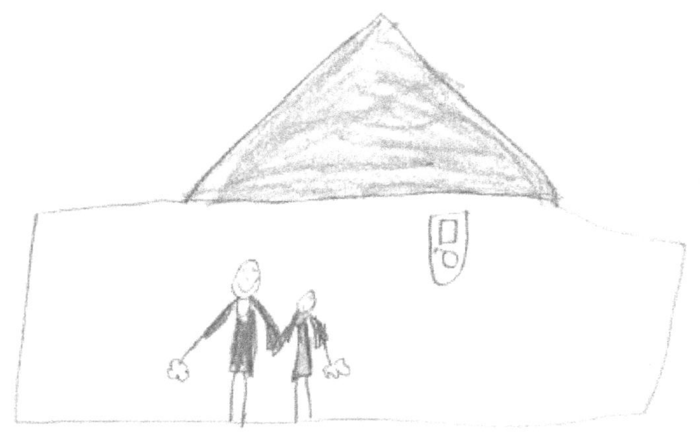

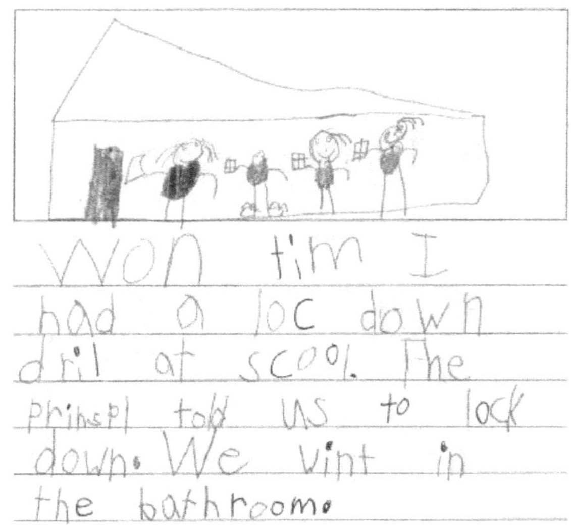

One time I had a lockdown drill at school. The principal told us to lockdown. We went in the bathroom.

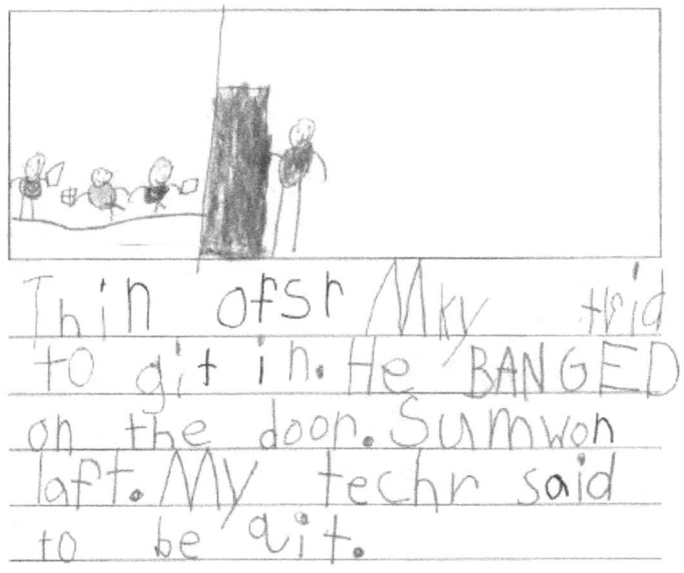

Then Officer McKee tried to get in. He BANGED on the door. Someone laughed. My teacher said to be quiet.

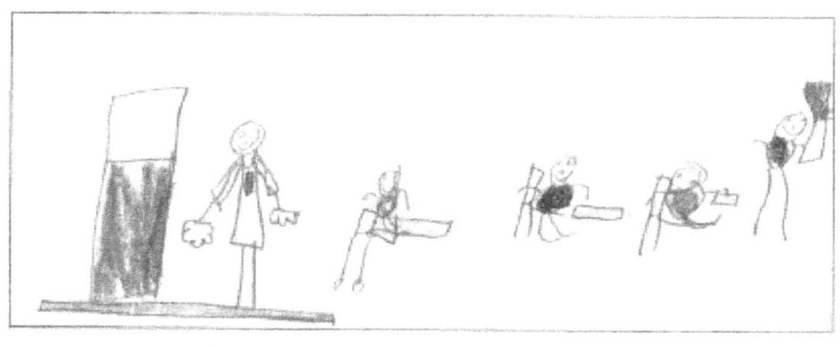

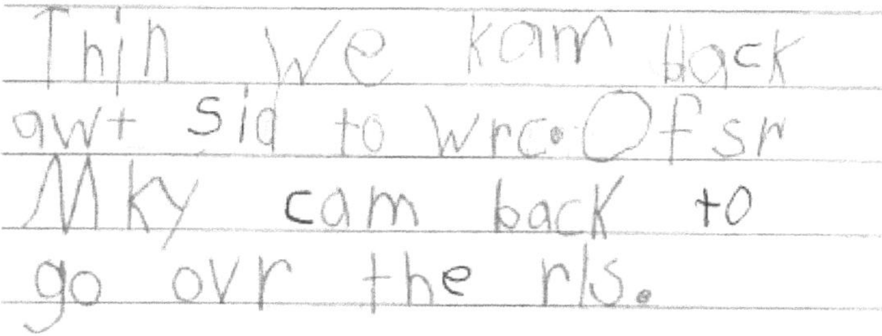

Then we came back outside to work. Officer McKee came back to go over the rules.

My Dog

Isaiah Johnson

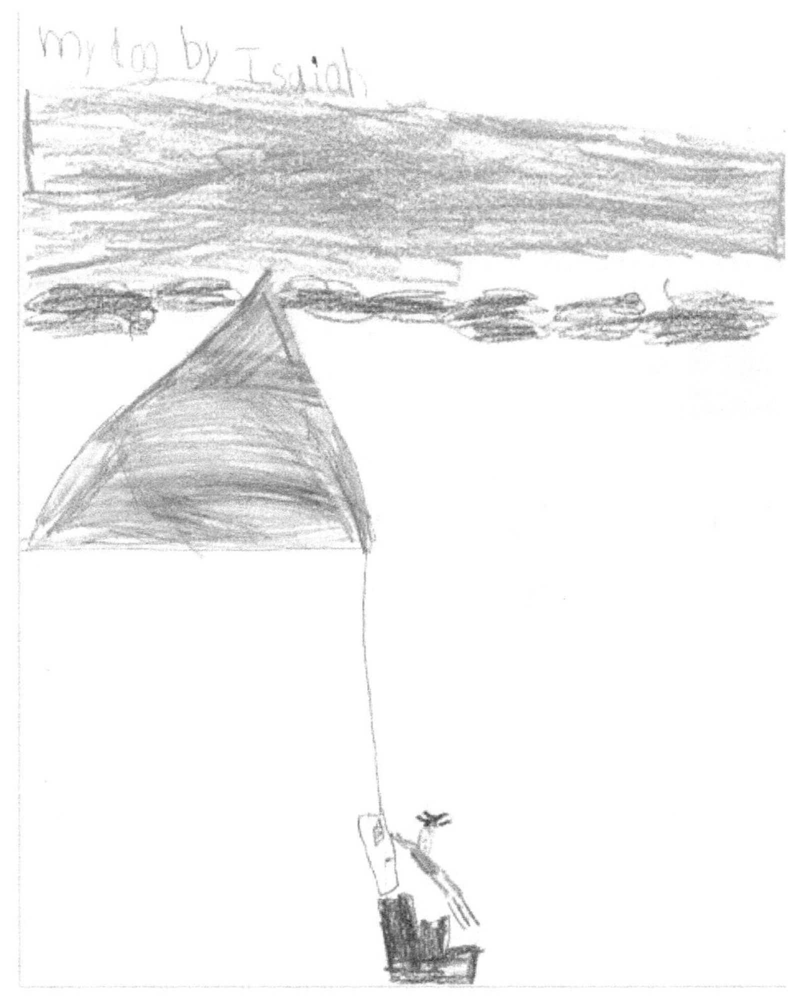

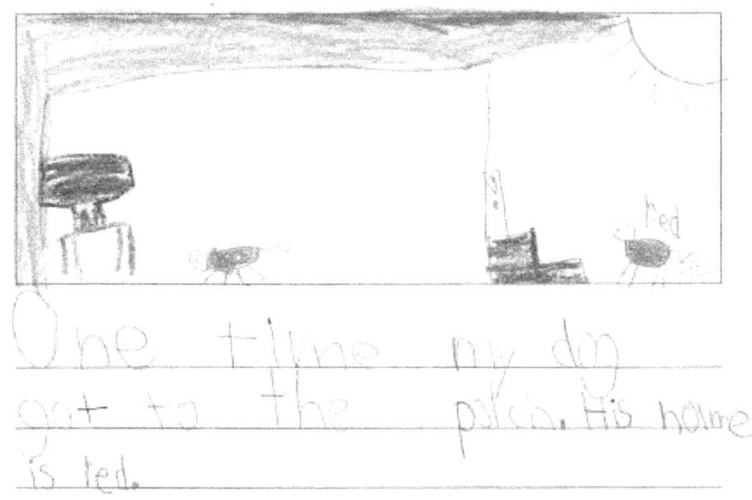

One time my dog got to the porch. His name is Red.

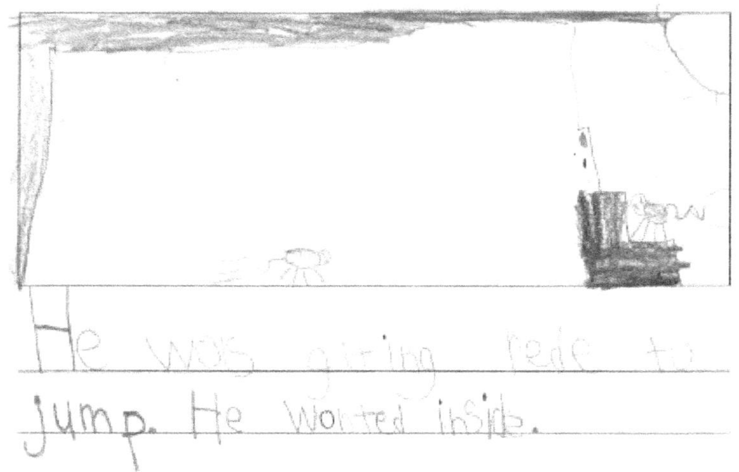

He was getting ready to jump. He wanted inside.

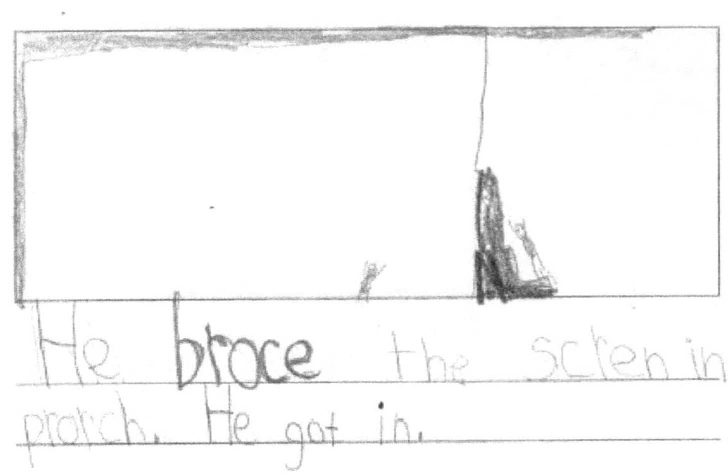

He broke the screen in porch. He got in.

I Went to the Pet Store

Issac Ogle

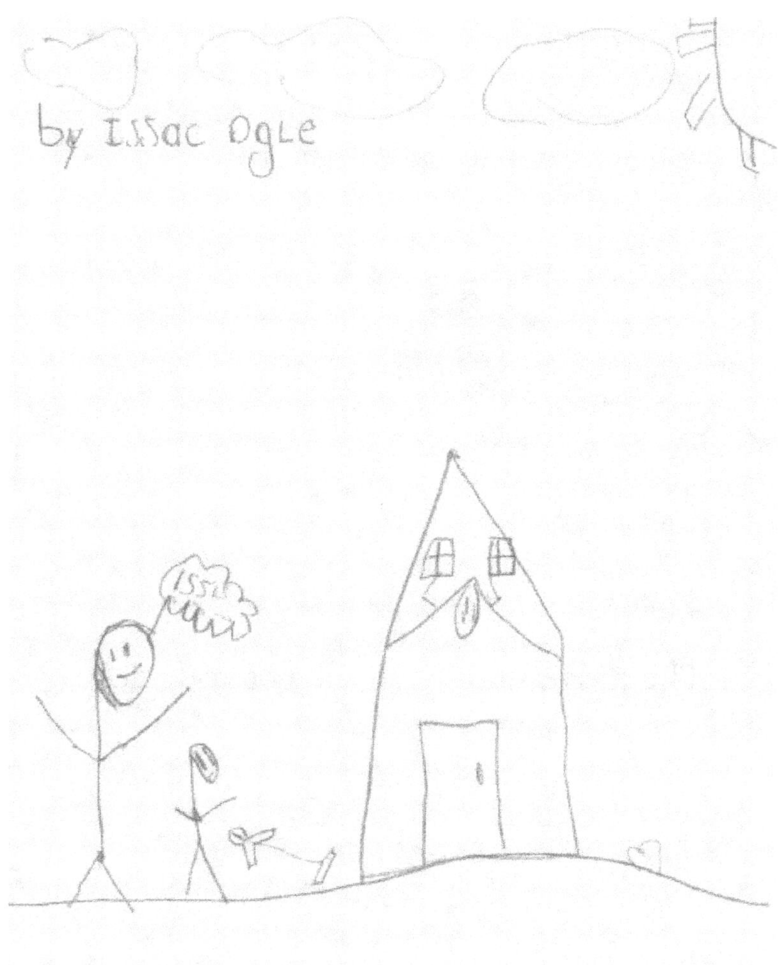

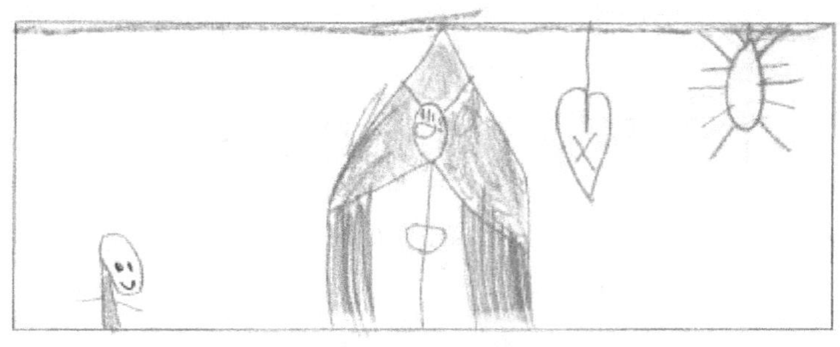

I went to the pet stor.

I went to the pet store.

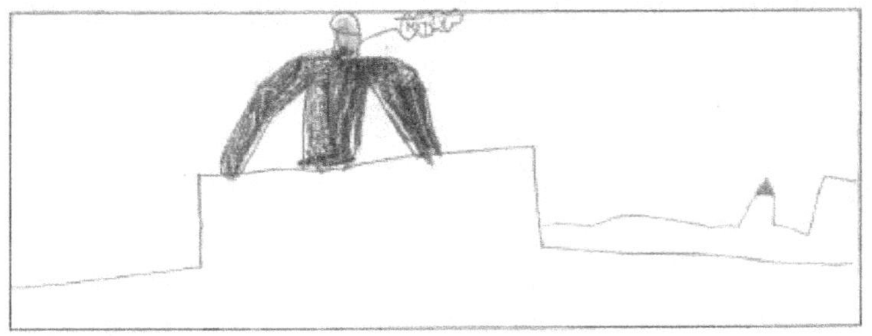

The judge said you will get your dog.

The judge said "you will get your dog."

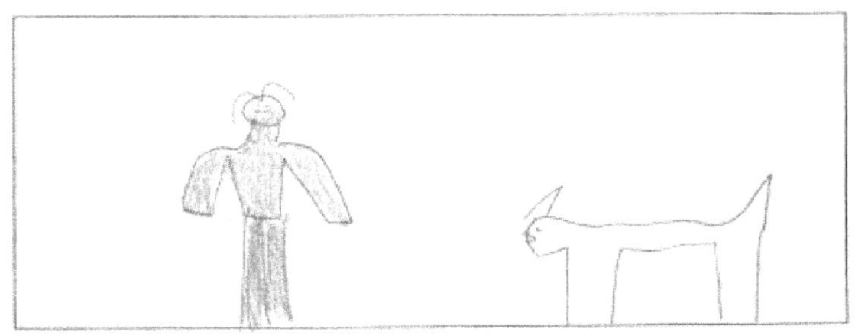

There is my dog.

There is my dog.

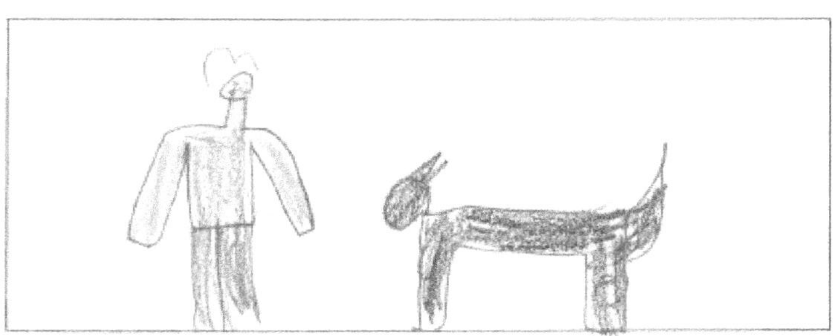

there is my uther.

There is my other.

I Read Lots of Books

Jayden Sanders

I red los of bucxs!
bi Jaydon

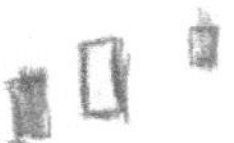

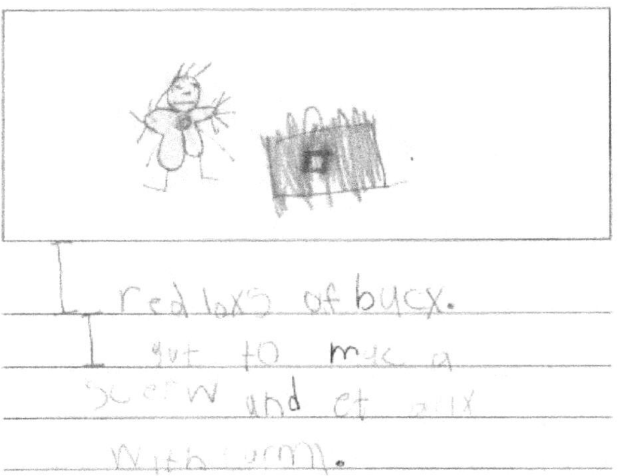

I read lots of books. I got to make a scarecrow and eat apples with caramel.

The Day I Went to the Apple Festival

Katelyn Guy

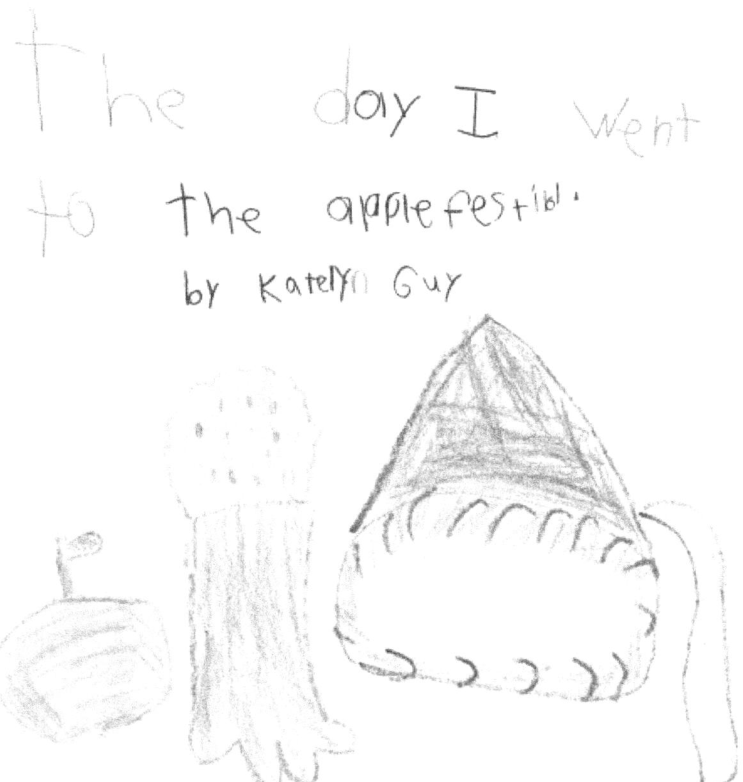

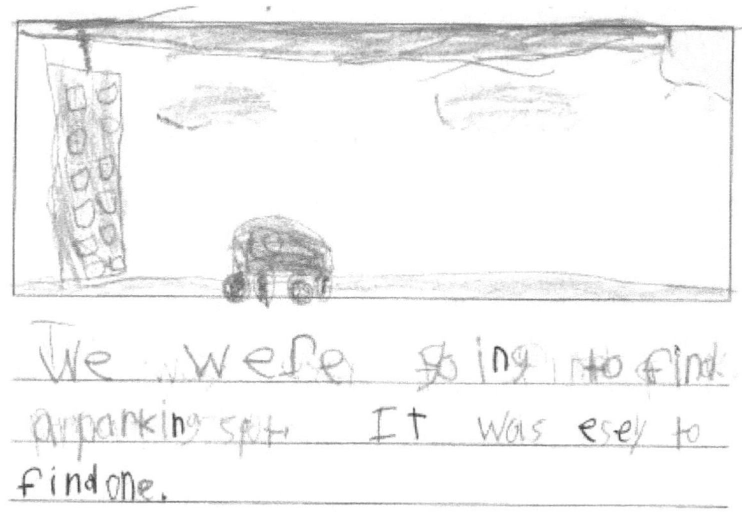

We were going to find a parking spot. It was easy to find one.

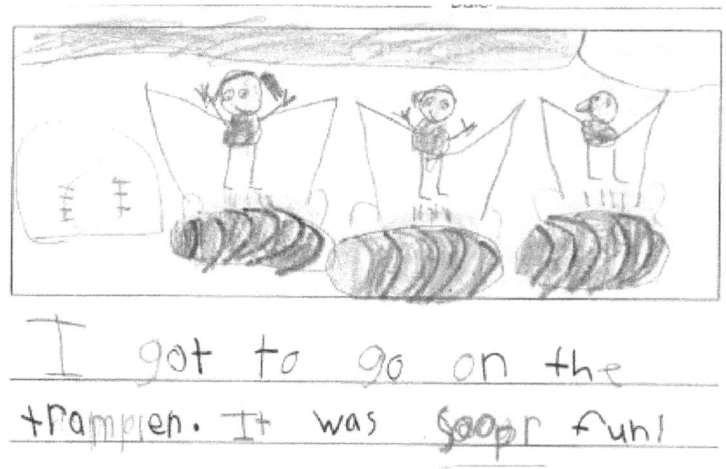

I got to go on the trampoline. It was super fun!

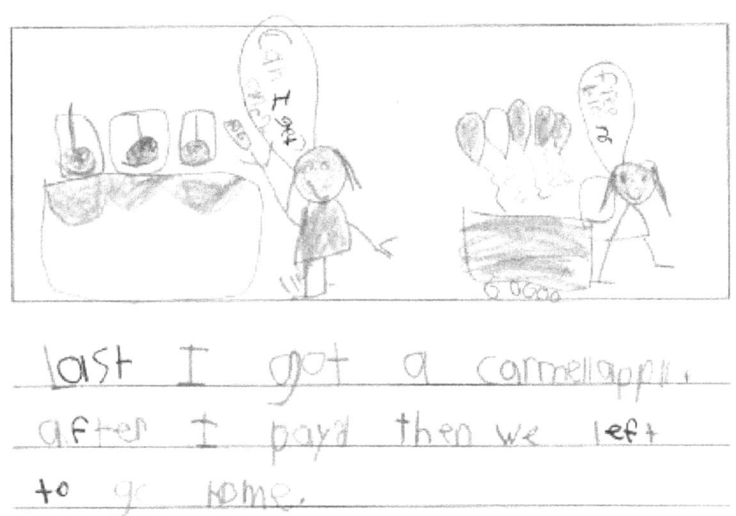

Last I got a caramel apple. After I paid then we left to go home.

Halloween Night

Kody McCleary

Hallwen Nit

by Kody McCleary

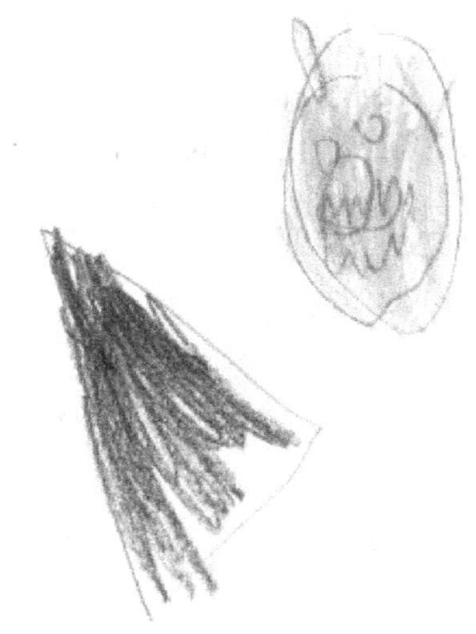

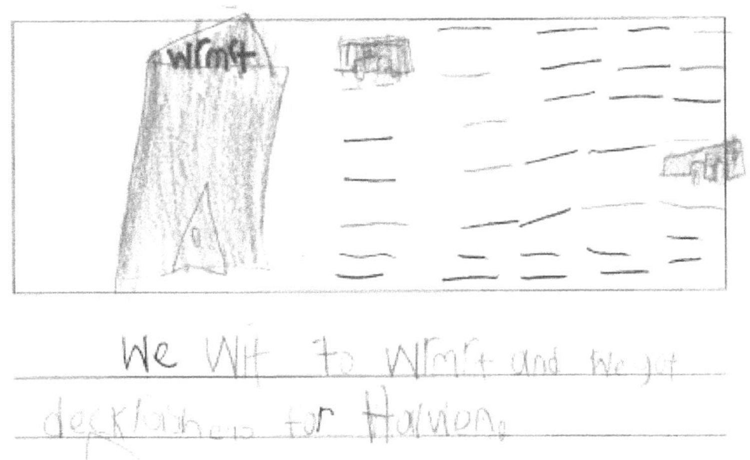

We went to Walmart and we got decorations for Halloween.

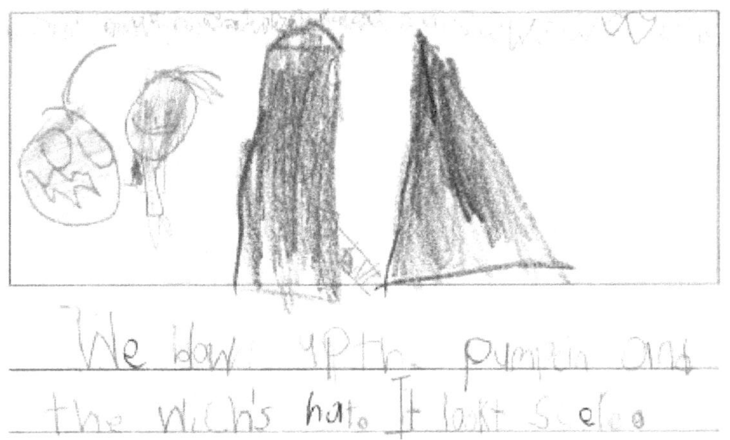

We blew up the pumpkin and the witch's hat. It looked scary.

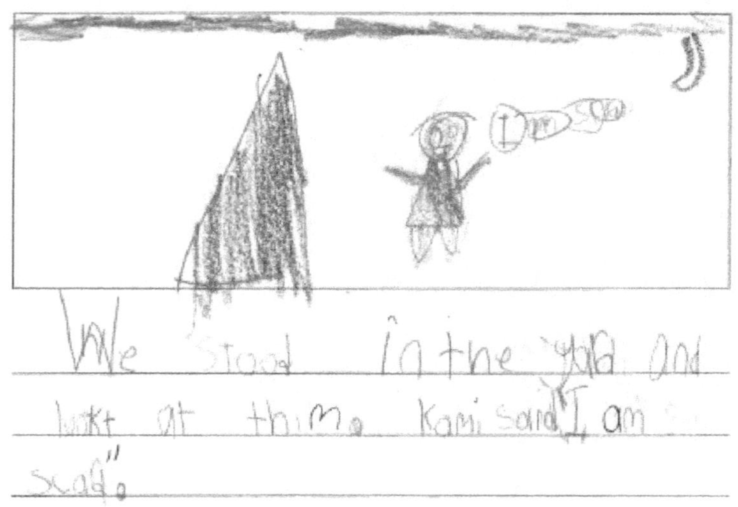

We stood in the yard and looked at them. Kami said, "I am scared."

The Runaway Brother!

Kyler Graham

The run away brather!

by: Kyler Graham

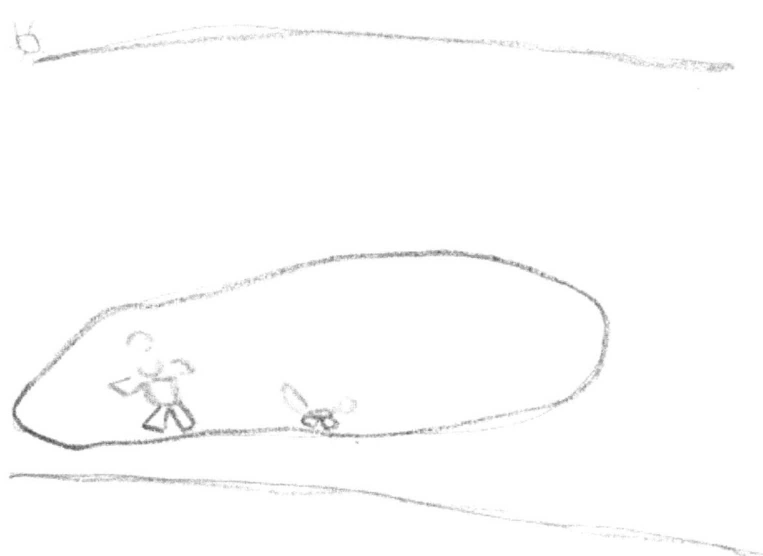

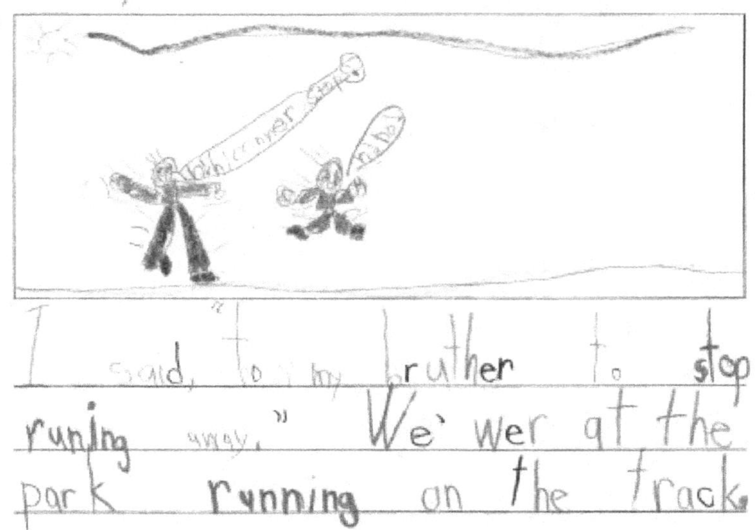

I said to my brother, "stop running away." We were at the park running on the track.

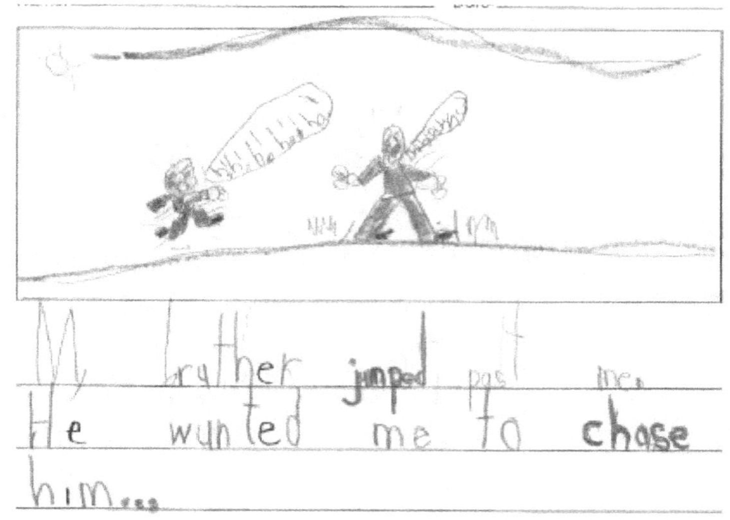

My brother jumped past me. He wanted me to chase him.

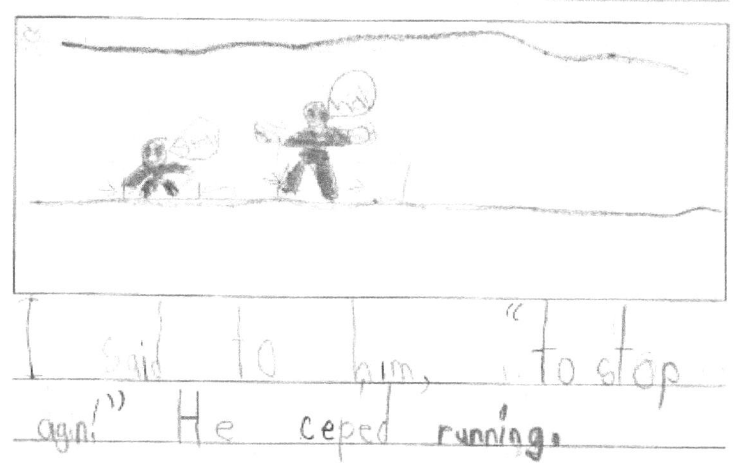

I said to him "stop" again. He kept running.

Fishing

Landon Edwards

Fishing

by Landon
Edwrs

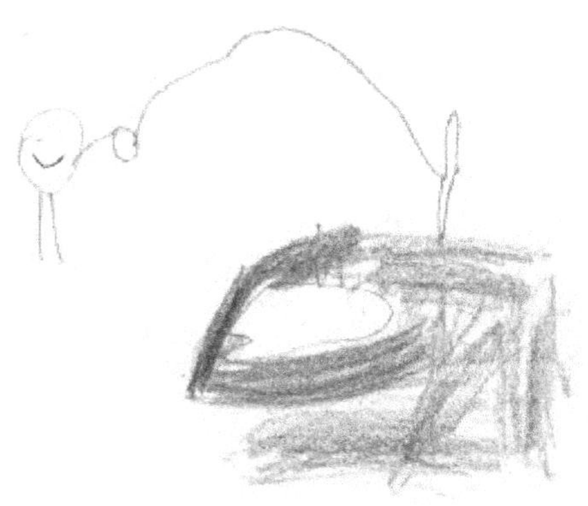

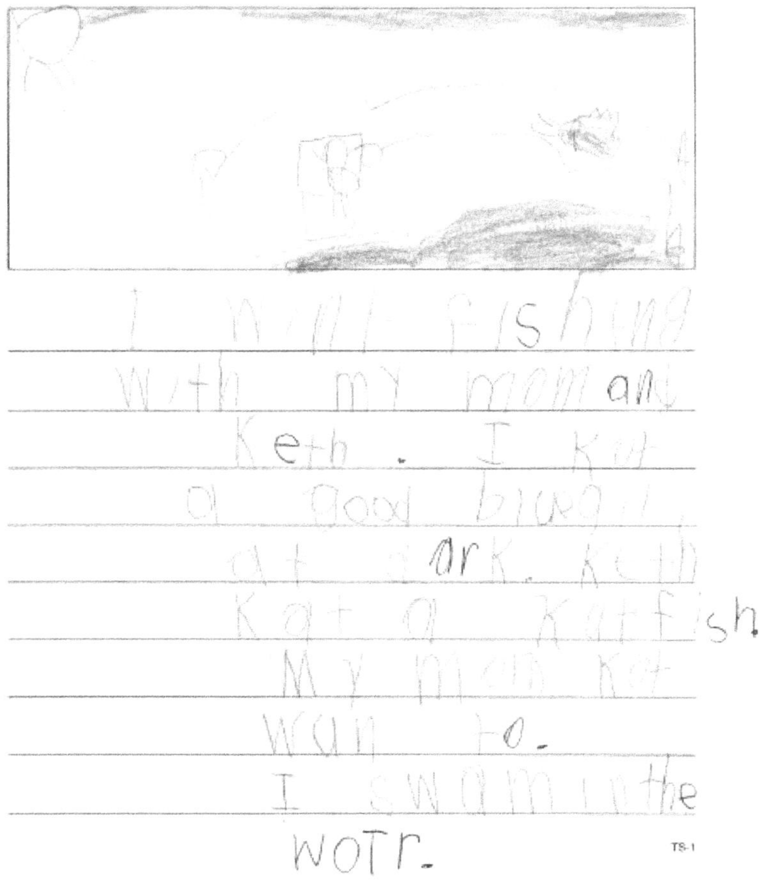

I went fishing with my mom and Keith. I caught a good bluegill at dark. Keith caught a catfish. My mom caught one too. I swam in the water.

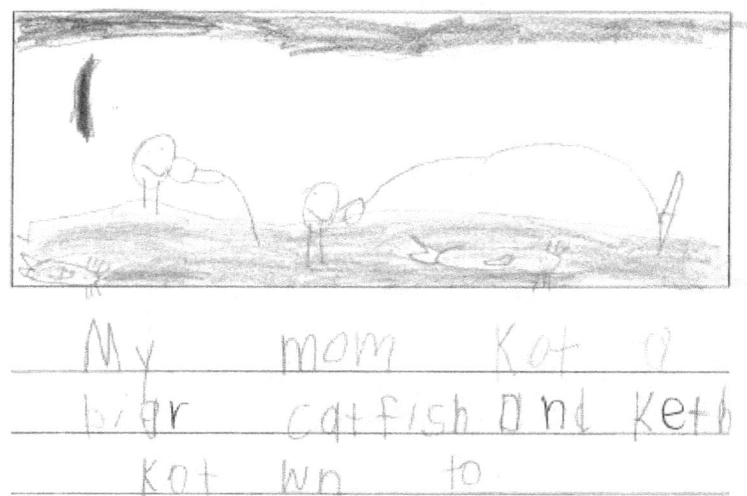

My mom caught a bigger catfish and Keith caught one too.

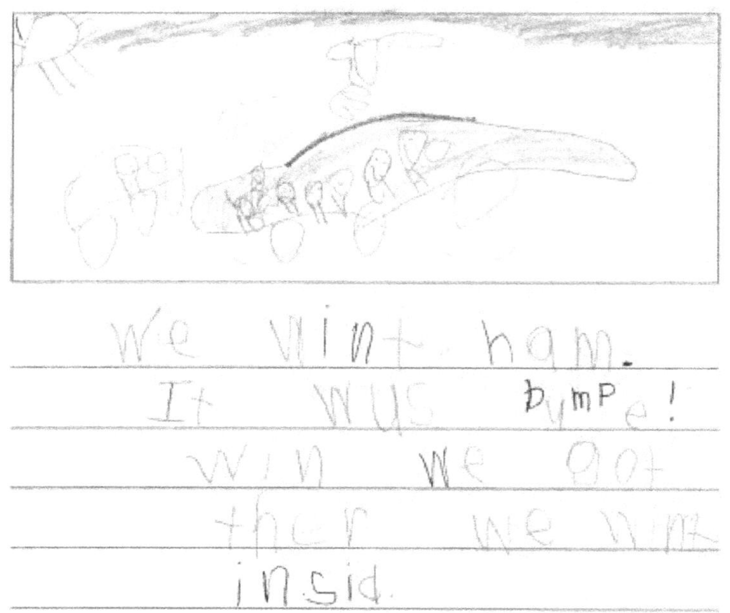

We went home. It was bumpy. When we got there, we went inside.

Missing My Oaklin

Maisey Green

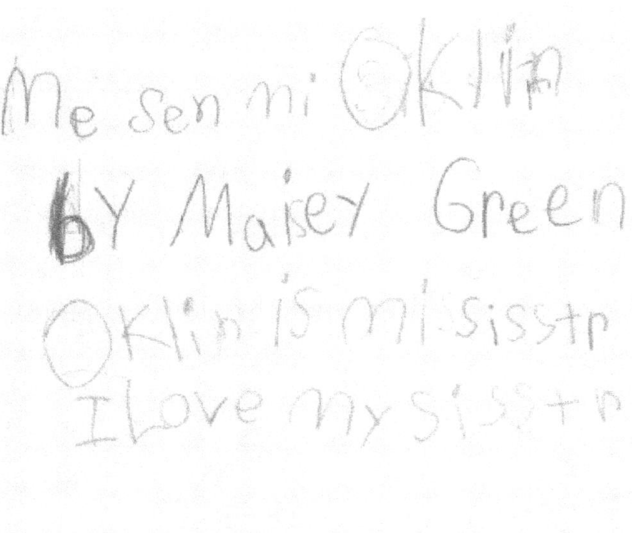

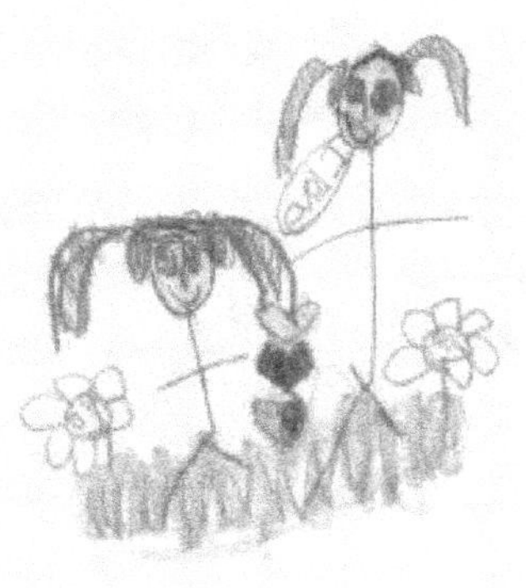

(Oaklin is my sister. I love my sister.)

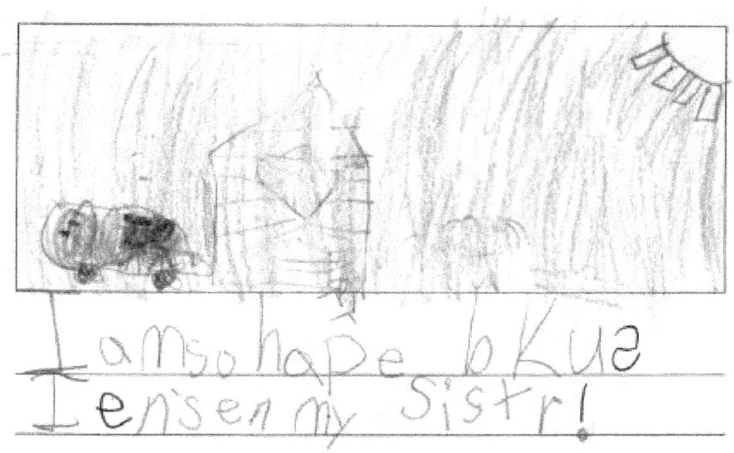

I'm so happy because I'm seeing my sister!

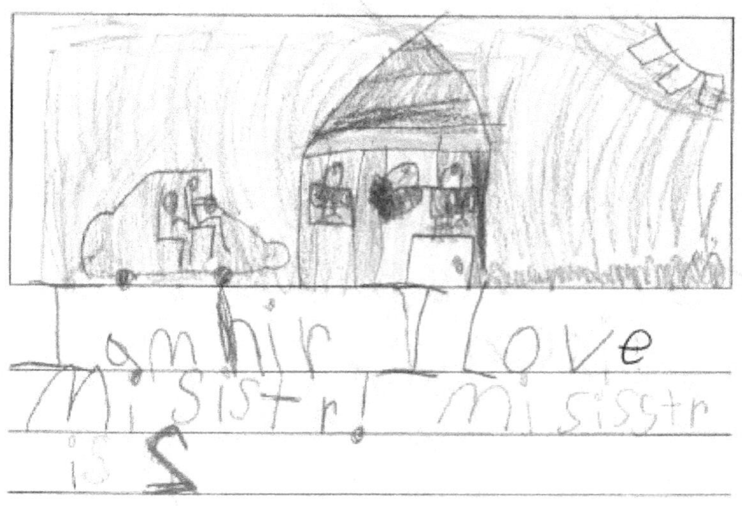

I am here. I love my sister! My sister is 2.

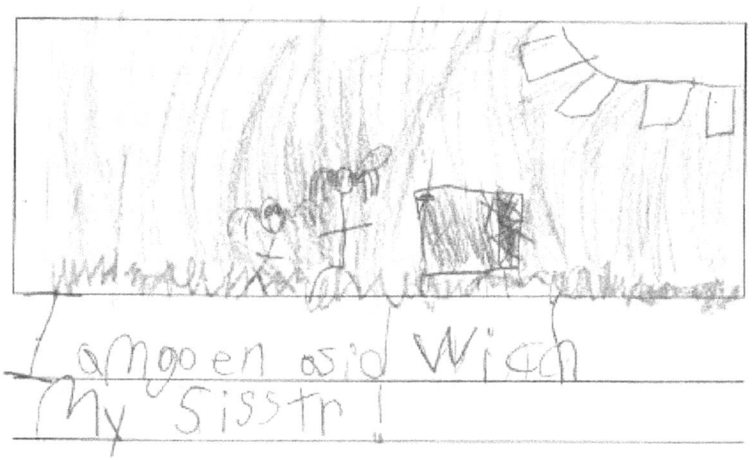

I am going outside with my sister!

Football

Maddox Cooper

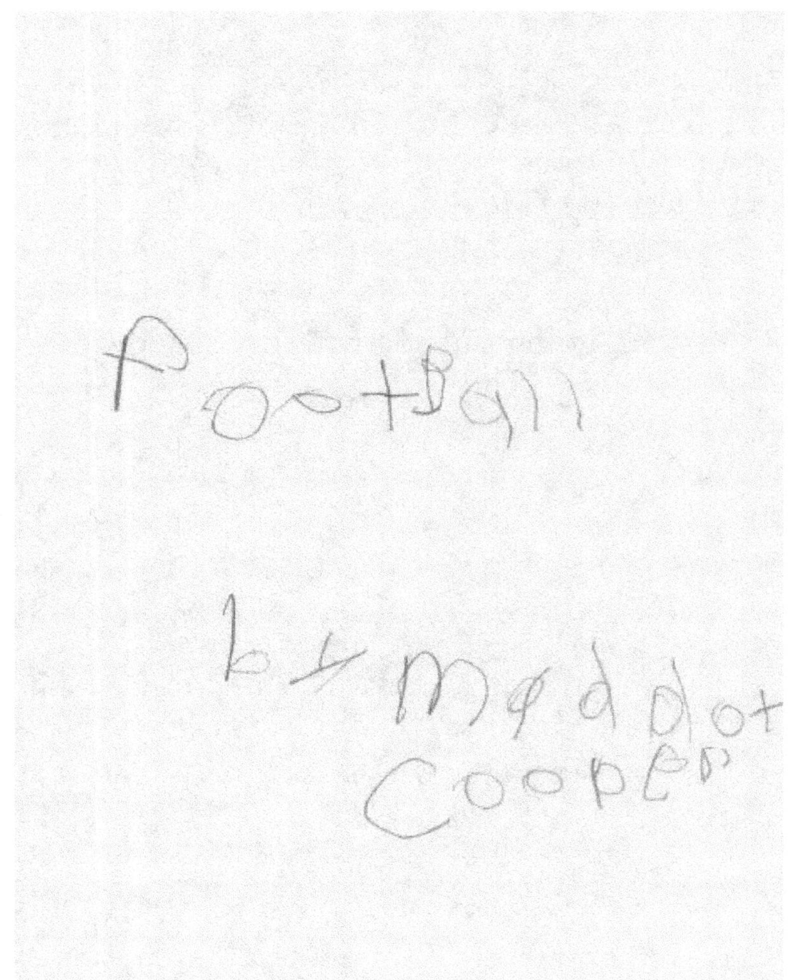

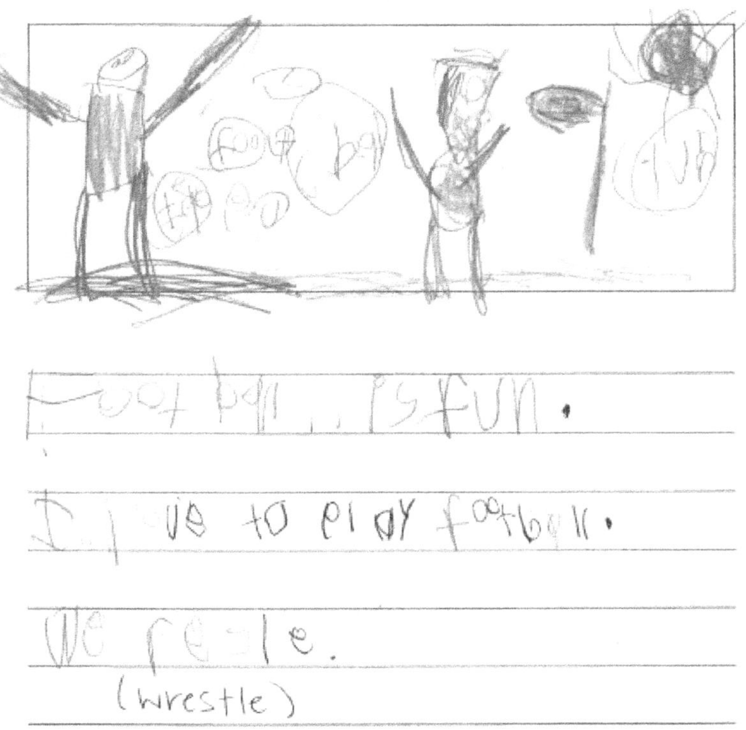

Football is fun. I love to play football. We wrestle.

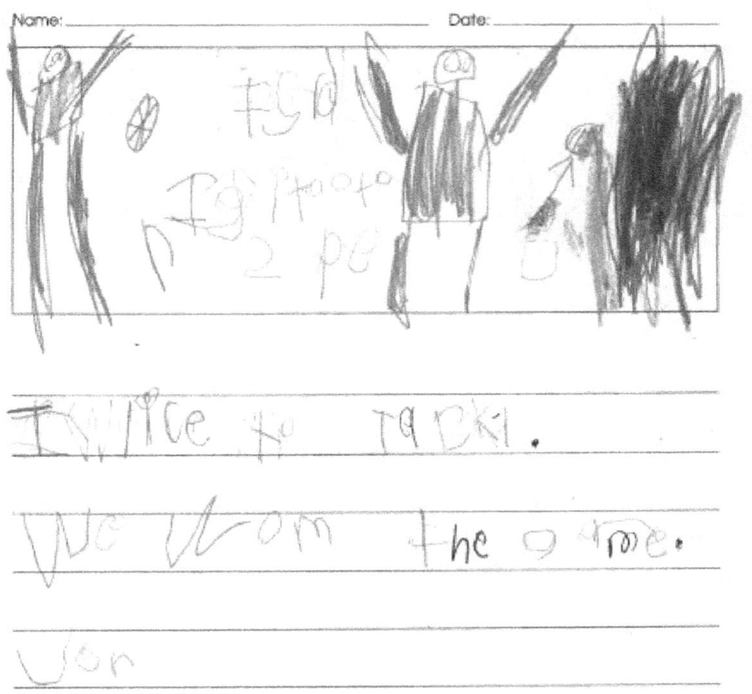

I like to tackle. We won the game.

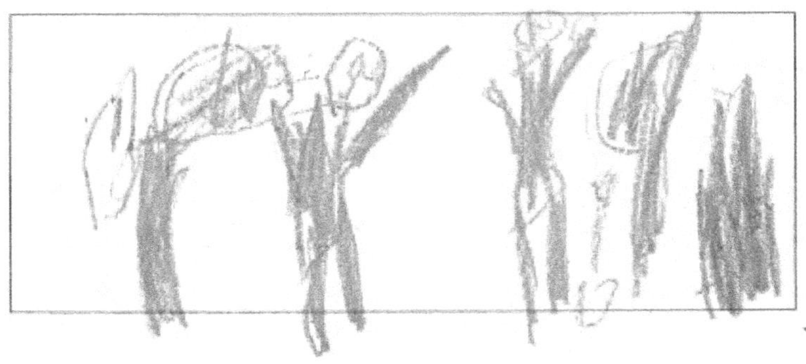

Going to the Park

Madyson Ledford

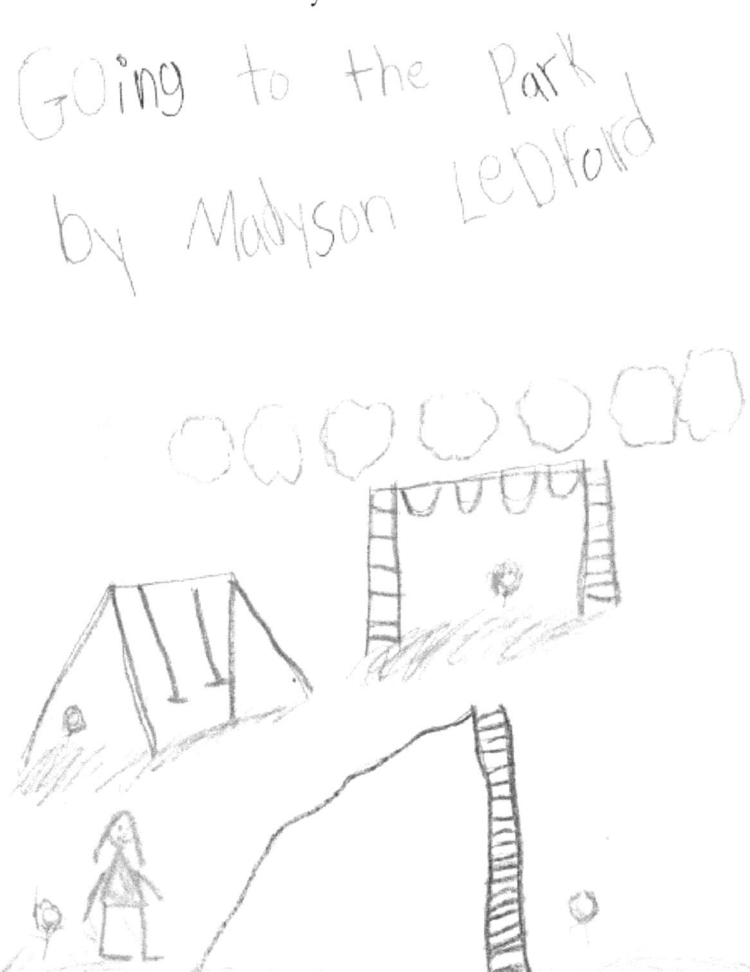

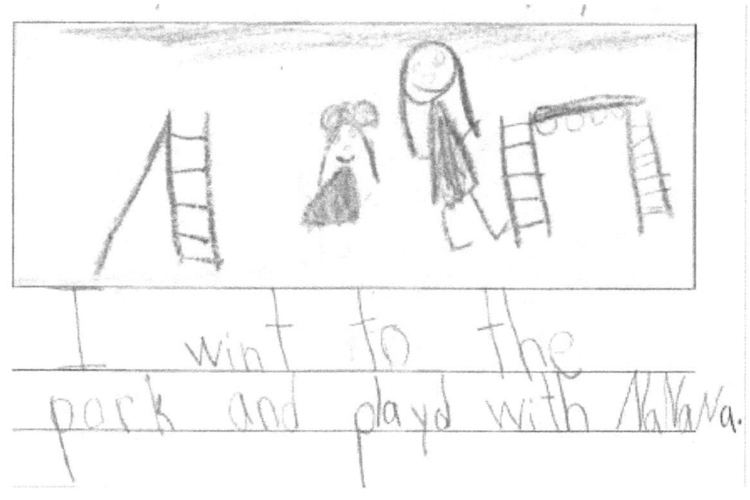

I went to the park and played with Nana.

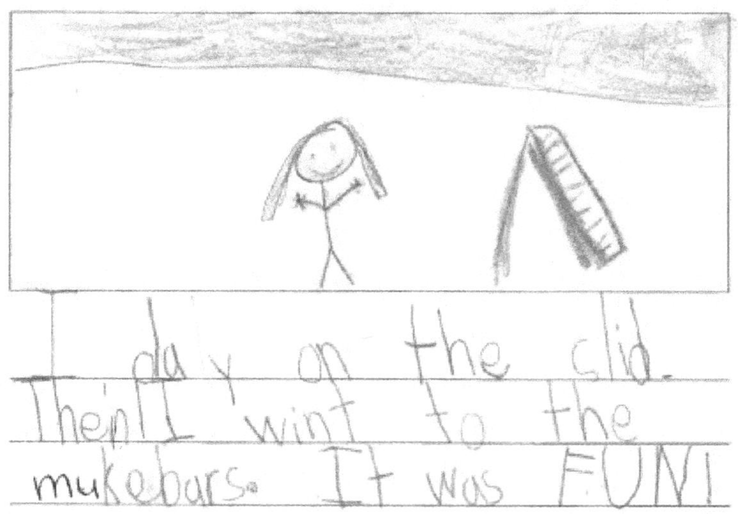

I played on the slide. Then I went to the monkey bars. It was FUN!

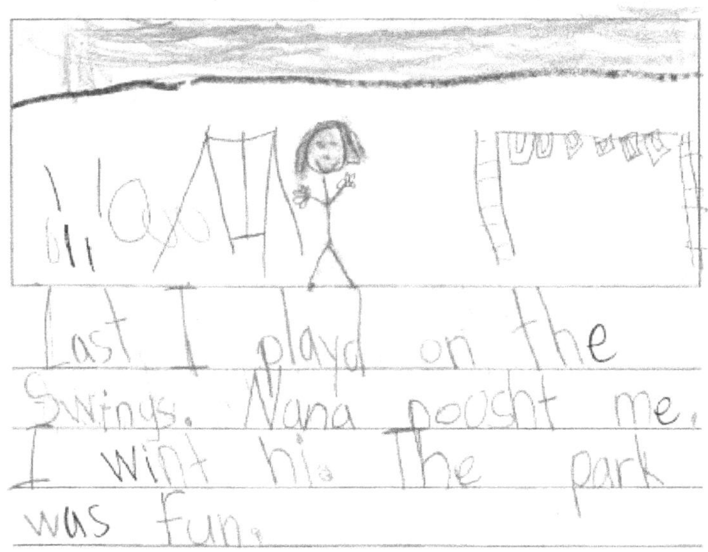

Last I played on the swings. Nana pushed me. I went high. The park was fun.

The Time We Washed Ron

Raegan LaDuke

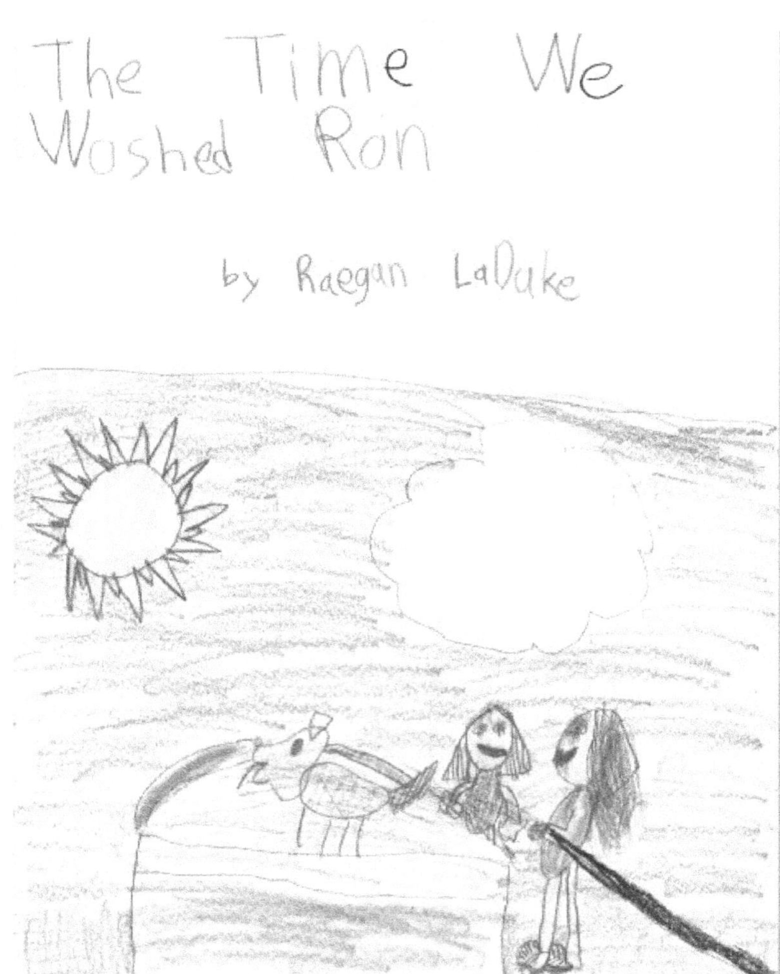

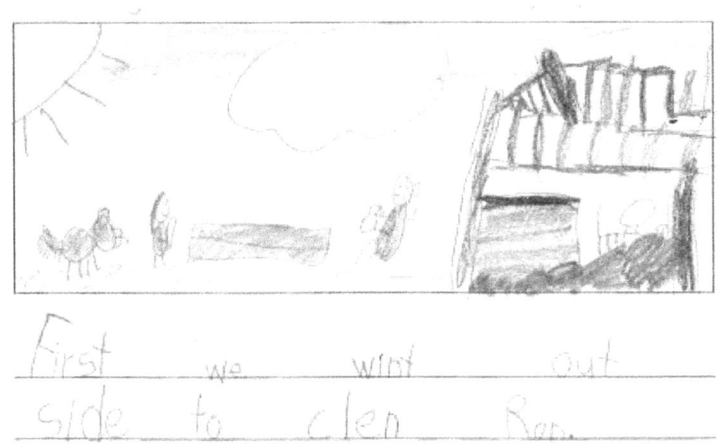

First we went outside to clean Ron.

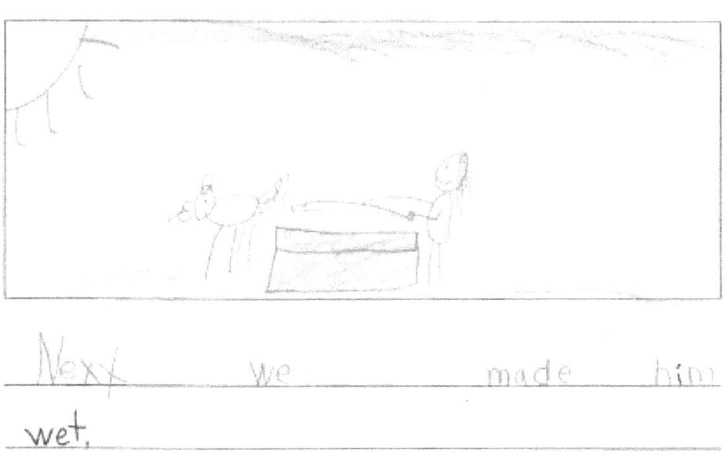

Next we made him wet.

Therd we sopet hem and Scredbt him. Forth we wosht the sope out of hi fir.

Then we soaped him and scrubbed him. Fourth we washed the soap out of his fur.

At the Park with Alivia and Ethan and Izca

Riley Trovato

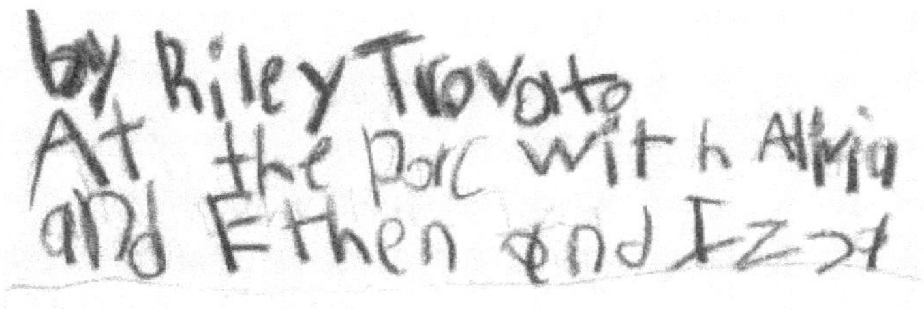

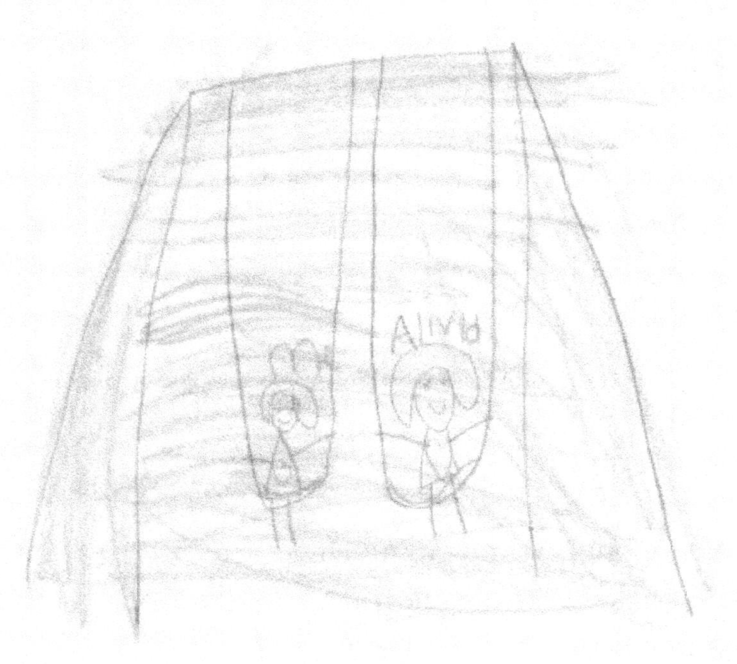

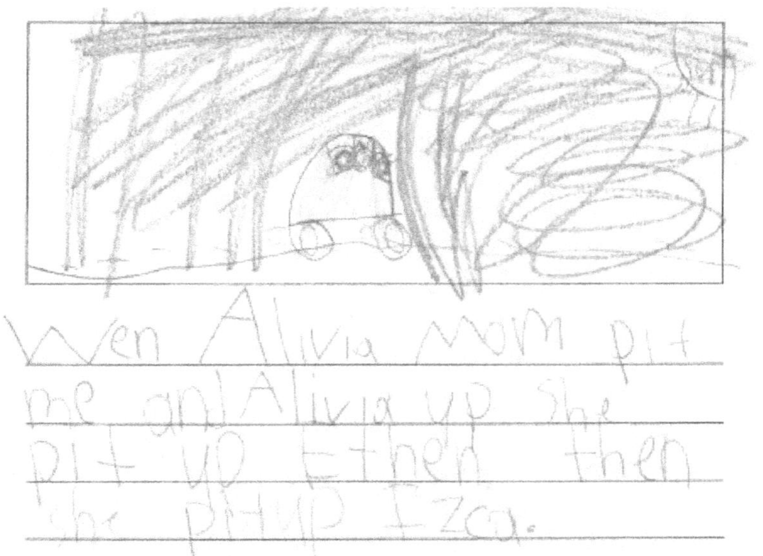

When Alivia's mom picked me and Alivia up she picked up Ethan then she picked up Izca.

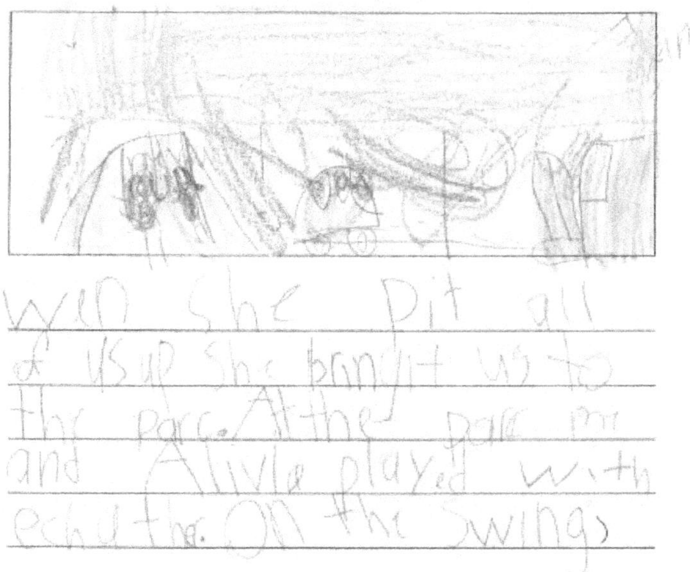

When she picked up all of us she brought us to the park. At the park me and Alivia played with each other on the swings.

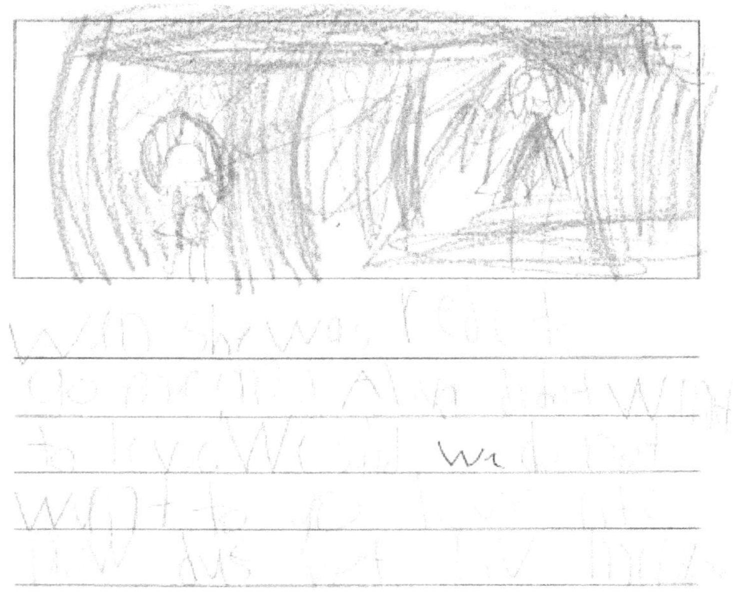

When she was ready to go me and Alivia didn't want to leave. We said, "we do not want to leave right now, just five more minutes."

Me and Papaw

Rock Burrell

Me and
PaPoll

by Rock

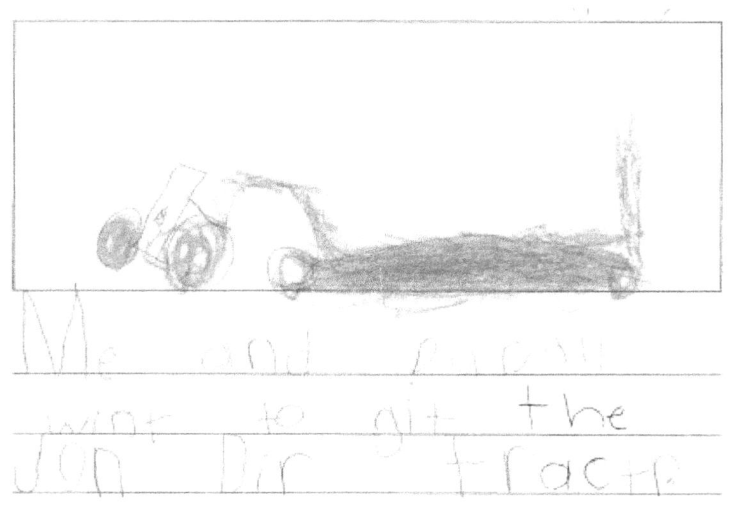

Me and Papaw went to get the John Deere tractor.

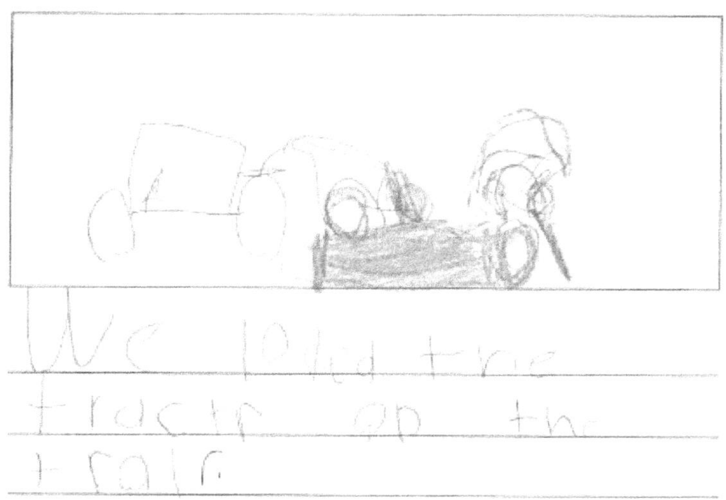

We loaded the tractor on the trailer.

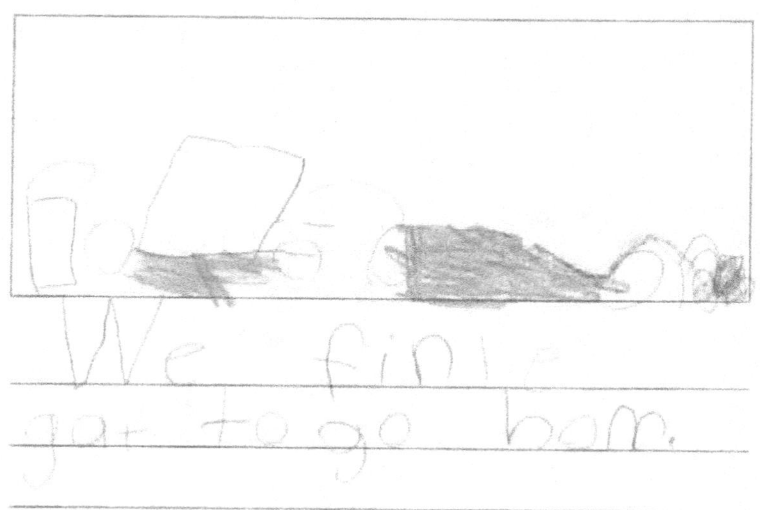

We finally got to go home.

When I Played Hill Climb Race 2

Silas Ellis

First I press the button. This is how I start my game.

Next I raced. I was happy.

Then I got in the first place! I felt really good!

Buster the Horse

Slade Marlow

I rode my horse at Mom's house. I had fun.

My horse's name is Buster. I made him jog.

He started to run fast. Coleman said, "Good job Slade."

My Horse is Trained!

Tenslee Norton

by Tenslee Norton

My hores is trained!

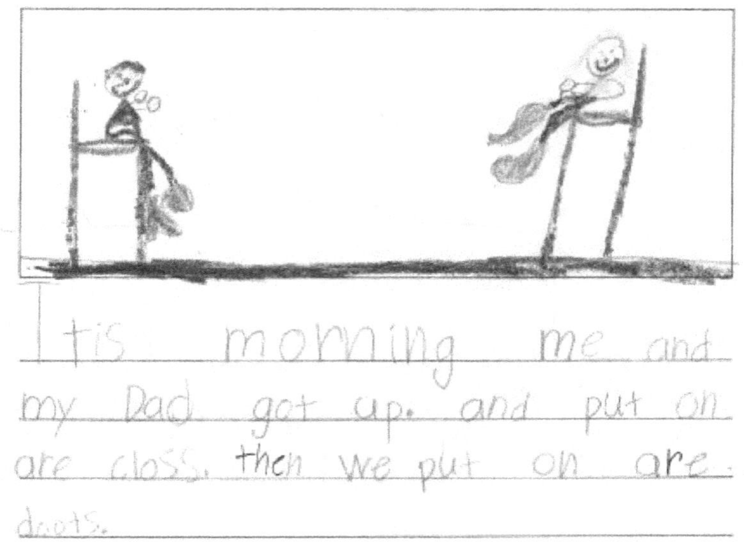

This morning me and my dad got up and put on our clothes. Then we put on our boots.

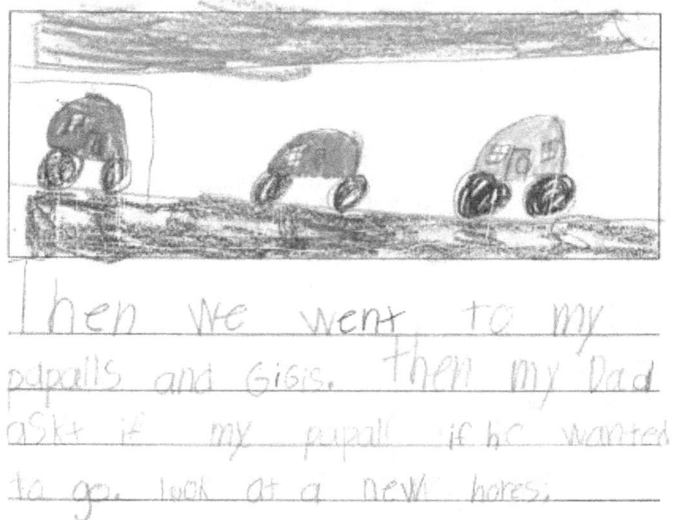

Then we went to my Papaw's and Gigi's. Then my dad asked my papaw if he wanted to go look at a new horse.

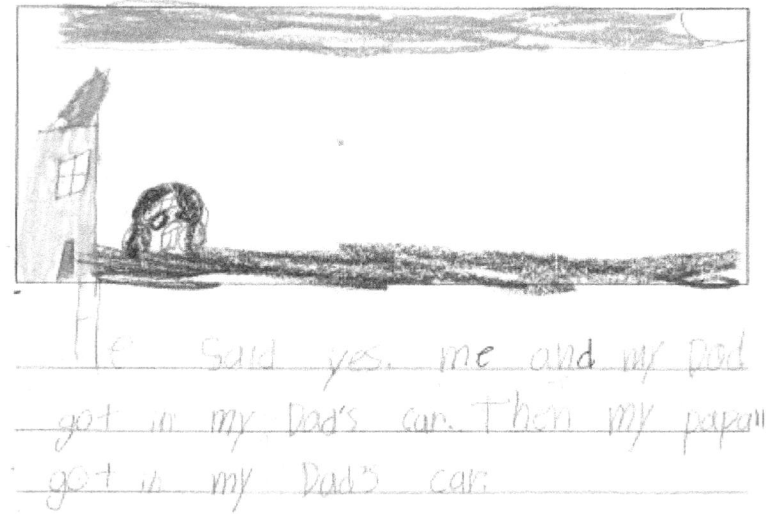

He said yes. Me and my dad got in my dad's car. Then my papaw got in my dad's car.

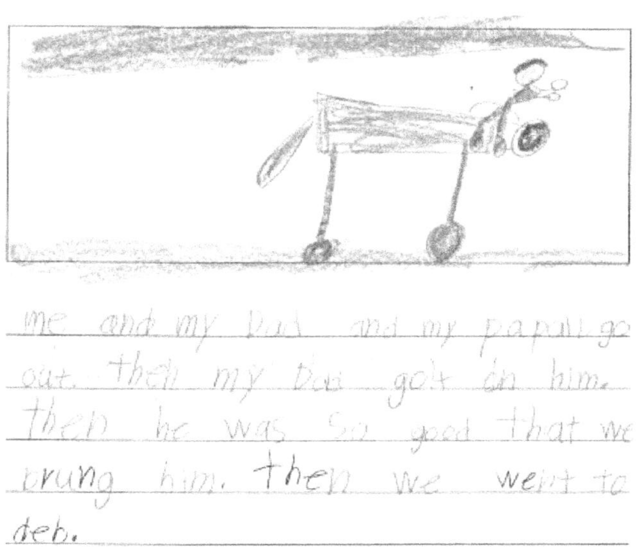

Me and my dad and my papaw got out. Then my dad got on him. Then he was so good that we brought him. Then we went to bed.

www.ingramcontent.com/pod-product-compliance
Lightning Source LLC
Chambersburg PA
CBHW071002180726
48291CB00004B/1400

* 9 7 8 1 9 4 9 8 8 8 3 3 1 *